KIDS *in the* LOOP

**CHICAGO ADVENTURES FOR KIDS
AND THEIR GROWN-UPS**

Anne Basye

CHICAGO
REVIEW
PRESS

Library of Congress Cataloging-in-Publication Data

Basye, Anne.
    Kids in the Loop : Chicago adventures for kids & their grown-ups /
Anne Basye.
        p.   cm.
    ISBN 1-55652-236-3 : $11.95
    1. Chicago (Ill.)—Guidebooks.   2. Chicago Region (Ill.)—
Guidebooks.   3. Family recreation—Illinois—Chicago—Guidebooks.
4. Family recreation—Illinois—Chicago Region—Guidebooks.
5. Children—Travel—Illinois—Chicago—Guidebooks.   6. Children—
Travel—Illinois—Chicago Region—Guidebooks.   I. Title.
F548.18.B39   1995
917.73'110443'083—dc20   94-49523
                                                                              CIP

First edition
Published by Chicago Review Press, Incorporated
814 North Franklin Street, Chicago, Illinois 60610
Printed in the United States of America
ISBN 1-55652-236-3

5 4 3 2 1

Contents

Acknowledgments

The African proverb "It takes a village to raise a child" also applies to the world of books and parents. It takes a neighborhood to support a parent, and it takes a city to write a book. I'm grateful to everyone who shared family adventures with me, to all the people and institutions who opened doors, answered questions, and supplied photographs, and most of all, to my companions in the parent trade, whose friendship I depend on so. Many thanks, all.

Preface

House work. School work. Home work. Work work. At the end of a grueling week, it's no wonder most families would rather hit the sofa than hit the road.

But now and then, wanderlust sneaks up on you. Maybe you wake up to a glittering day that just begs for a family field trip. Or a school holiday gives you a chance to let your hair down. Whatever the excuse, when the mood hits, *Kids in the Loop* can help you plan a wonderful family outing.

On these pages are places and family activities you may never have heard of, like the special kid's tours of the Frank Lloyd Wright Home and Studio, the Skybox for Rail Fans that overlooks Union Station, the half-day fossil hunt in the quarries near Camp Sagawau, Camp Sagawau itself, home to a lovely limestone canyon and a first-rate cross-country ski school, and all the great family overnights in the city's major institutions.

Other sites—the Kohl Children's Museum, or the Lincoln Park Zoo—you may already know like the back of your hand. But kids never tire of their favorite spots. And just because you've been someplace a hundred times doesn't mean your kids have. So what if you've seen the sights a million times, or you think they're just for tourists? See them with your kids, and you'll have a chance to get excited all over again about places you've been taking for granted—or worse yet, avoiding—for years.

So go ahead and visit the Sears Tower. Swallow your pride and try that double-decker bus. The farther you live from the Loop, the more curious your kids will be about it. Even if you're raising your kids right in the middle of it all—in Lake Point Tower or Dearborn Park, on Astor Street or Canal—your kids will leap at the chance to see their hometown as visitors do.

You'll soon find out that Chicago is a kid's kind of town.

A Few Words about Attention Span

Never underestimate the power of something simple to amaze your child, like a ride on the el, a visit to Buckingham Fountain, or the view from the Hancock Observatory.

(The corollary, of course, is that something you find wonderful will rouse your kids to a state of stunning indifference. Remember: patience, patience, patience!)

The simple something that amazes your child may not be the point of your journey—especially if it's self-guided. At the zoo, for instance, a young child may prefer watching a pigeon eat popcorn to looking at a lion, or chasing a squirrel to lifting up a hinged door to learn about the lion's habitat. Relax. No use crying over spilled pedagogy. Your child will have a good time anyway, and so should you. (Visit the zoo again when your kid is older and more interested in large mammals.)

On a guided tour, you can safely entrust your child's attention span to the docent leading the tour. Volunteers who give children's tours and talks know how to catch and keep a child's attention. Sit back and enjoy the ride!

A Few Words about Bathrooms

How well I remember family vacations when my mother used a paper towel to open bathroom doors in filthy gas stations. She often wished that someone would write a guidebook to the clean bathrooms of the West Coast.

In her honor, *Kids in the Loop* does its best to warn you when bathrooms are dirty, scarce, or missing. Fortunately, most of the family-oriented institutions included herein provide clean bathrooms, handicapped-accessible stalls, and changing tables.

A Few Words about Safety

Rising crime statistics and prime-time newscasts of urban calamities frighten every parent. Random gunfire and gang turf battles aside, most childhood injuries and deaths are *still* the result of accidental poisoning, falling, drowning, and car or bicycle collisions.

While most of the institutions mentioned in this book have taken many measures to ensure your family's safety, safeguarding your family is still your responsibility. On family outings, make sure kids follow basic safety practices like wearing seat belts and bicycle helmets, and looking both ways before crossing the street.

Chicago's complex traffic patterns make this last item especially important. Once, as we were crossing Ontario Street at Michigan Avenue, my son turned and ran back into the intersection to pick up a fallen object—directly into the path of a turning car. Fortunately, the incident ended with a stern lecture, not a frantic call to 911. It taught me not to overestimate my son's traffic sense and to always be on the alert for unexpected dangers.

To keep your kids from getting lost, make sure they know their first and last names, your first and last name, and their telephone number (including their area code). By elementary school, kids should know their address and their parents' work telephone numbers, too. Before you take your kids to a museum, agree on the steps each of you will take if you are separated. Point out the adults—security guards, ticket agents, people behind counters—who can help your child find you. With an older child, agree on a place to meet if you are separated.

Finally, parents who are distracted by a flock of children make ideal targets for pickpockets. In large institutions, restaurants, and on the street or the el, keep an eye on your purse or wallet.

On Beyond Zebra

Opportunities for excursions regularly present themselves in the *Chicago Tribune, Chicago Sun-Times*, the *Daily Herald*, the *Southtown Economist*, and Chicago neighborhood papers. The alert parent will find a gold mine of ideas in the monthly newspaper, *Chicago Parent*, where Chicago museums, theaters, and schools often send press releases about special events. Another good source is *MOMents*, a monthly newsletter for working parents whose back-page calendar offers a great roundup of seasonal events and activities.

When you're trolling for new places to go and new things to do, remember that not every expedition has to be major. Humble events like spaghetti dinners, Boy Scout pancake breakfasts, Park District water shows, and parish carnivals can be cheap, rewarding, and fun.

Best wishes for many great Chicago adventures!

I

Toddlin' Around Town

When it comes to seeing sights, Chicago kids have it made. Forget about boring cars and tired feet. In Chicago, you can see the city by boat, train, horse-drawn carriage, bus, or trolley. You can even tour Chicago by elevator, if that elevator happens to ascend the world's tallest building.

So take the kids and visit the Sears Tower. Try the double-decker bus. Let someone in a top hat drive you around town in a carriage. Or set aside all modesty and join your kids in peering at the Loop from a pirate's spyglass.

'Round and About the Loop El Tour

All the secrets of the Loop in just forty-five minutes? It's possible on the 'Round and About the Loop el tour, conducted Saturday afternoons from May through September. Great for older children who are studying Chicago history and fun for tots who just like riding trains, this tour offers something for everybody.

Explaining everything about the Loop takes three circumlocutions. The first time around, your family will learn about the history of the el system in Chicago. On the second loop, you'll

1

hear the history of the buildings along the inner loop of the el; on the third, you'll learn about the buildings on the outer loop. You'll have plenty of time to point out your favorite sights to your kids before the question-and-answer period that wraps up the trip.

Get tickets at the *'Round and About the Loop* exhibit inside the Cultural Center, where you can watch a seven-minute presentation on the Loop's history and pick up a map that indicates absolutely everything of interest in the Loop, from pedways and outdoor sculpture to notable buildings like the Monadnock and the Rookery. (This one's a keeper—take your copy home and file it away for future adventures in the Loop.)

Tickets in hand, your family can climb the stairs and board the train at the Randolph and Wabash Station. (If you need wheelchair access, call ahead and arrange to board via the elevator at the Clark and Lake station.) This is a great way to get over to the Sears Tower, too; on your third lap around the Loop, you can get off at Quincy Station and take a short walk to the Skydeck.

An el ride is always a treat for kids, and this one is very special, taking your kids around and around the most exciting part of the entire el system and letting them discover for themselves the secrets of the Loop landscape. Their excitement will rub off on you—even if you've been riding the el so long that you usually pass through the Loop in a trance!

'Round and About the Loop
Chicago Cultural Center
78 E. Washington Street
744-7590

The Little Red Trolley and the Big Red Bus

Most of the best-known Chicago "sights" are in the downtown area, where parking costs a fortune and dozens of city blocks can separate famous destinations.

By investing in day-long passes for one of the tourist trolleys or buses that toddle around town, you'll delight your kids and spare everyone's temper.

The Chicago Trolley Company can swiftly move you from one Chicago highlight to another for a fairly modest sum (modest, that is, compared to the money you'd spend parking your car again and again). As you travel, your kids will be entertained by talented driver/actors who add a liberal dose of wit and humor to their running commentary about Chicago and its wonders.

The trolley runs seven days a week from 10:00 A.M. until 5:00 P.M. (6:00 P.M. in the summer), stopping at major institutions like the Sears Tower, North Pier, Navy Pier, the Water Tower, the Art Institute, and the lakefront museums. A full-day pass lets you get on or off at any stop, so an ambitious family could start at the Sears Tower, have lunch in the food court at North Pier, and then spend the afternoon at the Field Museum before returning to its car.

In the summer, the trolleys are open air; in winter, they're sealed up tight to keep your kids warm, dry, and happy on your downtown adventure. The nine-mile tour of the city costs $10 for adults and $7 for kids. (Kids under 3 are free.) You can buy tickets at any of the stops along the way, and upgrade to a two-day pass for a mere $3 more.

The bright red double-decker buses follow pretty much the same route and offer kids the exciting chance to sit way up on the top level of a real English bus. (Your kid won't want to sit anywhere else.)

Like the trolleys, the double-decker buses operate 365 days a year, stopping only if a blizzard immobilizes the city. In inclement weather, buses run less often. But on the bright side, on cold days the company brings out its deluxe buses, which are heated, enclosed, and have comfortably upholstered seats. There are no public bathrooms on the bus, but your friendly bus driver can probably tell you where the closest one can be found.

These drivers know everything. They know the basic Chicago stats, a smattering of history, and a little ethnic and demographic data. They can point out filming locations of famous movies, recommend good family restaurants, or tantalize your kids with inside info, like why a Wilson basketball sits on top of Michael Jordan's restaurant. And the drivers are happy to include your kids in their patter if you clue them in on names and special interests first. Ditto for birthdays: if you tell your driver, your kid will be astonished to hear a birthday salute on the PA system.

Some double-decker buses have wider exits and lower steps to allow wheelchair access. (Call first to find out when these models will be running.) Passengers can sit in their wheelchairs on the lower level or, if they have some mobility, can store their wheelchairs on the bottom level and enjoy the view from the top. Strollers can also be stashed on the lower level.

One complete circuit plus a day's on-and-off privileges costs $10 for adults and $6 for kids under 11. (A tour with no stops costs $7.) During summer, the buses run from 9:00 A.M. to about 9:00 P.M.; during winter, from 9:00 A.M. to 4:00 P.M. Kids on laps ride free.

Chicago Trolley Company
738-0900

Chicago Motor Coach Company
922-8919

Horse and Carriage Rides

Favored by honeymooners and visiting Rotarians, horse and carriage rides are also a special treat for children. A $35, thirty-minute trip can take your family down Michigan Avenue, over to Lake Shore Drive, or in and out the narrow side streets of Streeterville and the Gold Coast.

You'll find most of the horses and carriages in the vicinity of Water Tower Place. Patient drivers will let your child say hello to the horses, or even feed them carrots, before they trot off. If you want to travel during daylight hours, schedule your trip for the weekend; on weekdays, rides begin at 7:00 P.M., although the

Noble Horse does offer tours from noon to 4:00 P.M. on week-days.

During your ride, expect to enjoy the sights and your children's wonder, but don't expect to be entertained by your driver. While she can point out a few prominent sights, your driver will be preoccupied with guiding her horse down crowded urban streets. And during the winter enclosed carriages make conversing with your driver nearly impossible.

Antique Coach
Leaves from Michigan Avenue and Huron Street
735-9400

Chicago Horse & Carriage
Leaves from Southeast corner of Michigan Avenue and
Pearson Street
944-6773

The Noble Horse
Leaves from Pearson Street and Michigan Avenue, next to
the Park Hyatt
266-7878

One If by Land, Two If by Sea

In Chicago, you can strain your neck staring up at skyscrapers, or unsettle your stomach gazing at humans, hundreds of fright-ening feet below. For a gentler perspective, your family can enjoy observing Chicago from a boat deck.

Two major cruise companies departs from the Chicago River at Michigan Avenue. Wendella Sightseeing Boats embarks from the north side of the river, in front of the Wrigley Building; Mercury Cruiseline leaves from the south bank. Both compa-nies offer one-, one-and-a-half-, and two-hour cruises that take passengers along the Chicago River and out onto Lake Michigan.

Most likely to hold your child's attention is the one-hour cruise, which travels east from Michigan Avenue, through the lock, and out onto Lake Michigan. Along the way, your kids will hear all about Chicago history and architecture, learn some fun facts about our town, and enjoy the thrilling experience of feeling the boat rise and sink in the Chicago lock. In fact, unless your family owns a boat, a Wendella or Mercury boat ride is the *only* way your kids can see the lock firsthand, since there is no way for the general public to walk out to it.

Wendella offers one-hour tours at 2:15, 5:30, and 9:00 P.M.; Mercury offers them at 5:00, 9:00, 10:00, and 11:00 P.M. Adults pay $8; children under 11 pay $4. Kids under 3 are free on the Wendella line; Mercury charges for kids over 18 months old. Wendella will stash your stroller at the dock for free; Mercury lets you bring it on board. Both lines have bathrooms on board and offer cruises from May 1 through mid-October.

For an even shorter voyage, try Shoreline Sightseeing Cruises. These boats leave from three piers along the lake—at the John G. Shedd Aquarium, the Adler Planetarium, and Buckingham Fountain—and cruise north to the Hancock Building and back without traveling up the river. During the thirty-minute cruise, you hear a prerecorded lecture on Chicago history, Great Lakes ecology, and the secrets behind the locks, the offshore water cribs, and the Chicago water purification system. This is a good choice if you are hosting international visitors, because a script of the lecture is available in twelve foreign languages. (Shoreline management says it adds a new language every year.)

Shoreline boats run from May through September. From 11:15 A.M. until 6:15 P.M., boats leave every thirty minutes from the aquarium and the planetarium docks, making a cruise the perfect way to cap off a visit to the Field Museum, the aquarium, or the planetarium. Evening tours depart Buckingham Fountain every thirty minutes from 7:15 until 11:15 P.M. Shoreline also offers a shuttle service between Navy Pier and the aquarium; call for prices and times.

Shoreline boats have bathrooms and soft-drink machines and are accessible to strollers and wheelchairs *except* at the planetarium dock. Tickets for adults are $6; kids under 12 are $3. Group rates are available.

Wendella Sightseeing Boats
400 N. Michigan Avenue
337-1446

Mercury Cruiseline
Michigan Avenue and Lower Wacker Drive
332-1368

Shoreline Sightseeing Cruises
Departures from the Shedd Aquarium, the Adler
Planetarium, and Buckingham Fountain
222-9328

● ●

The Shortest Boat Trip of All

If your child hungers for a boat ride but can't take a full hour on board, disguise yourselves as commuters and travel between 4:45 and 5:27 P.M. That's when the Wendella line ferries commuters from Michigan Avenue to Madison Street to catch suburban trains. There's no narration and you don't go anywhere near the locks, but a round-trip lasts a mere fifteen minutes—seven minutes dock to dock, with time for boarding—and costs only $1 each way. Boats depart every ten minutes during rush hour, Monday through Friday.

● ●

Yo Ho Ho and a Bottle of Pop

Pirates on the Chicago River? Sure. Thursday through Sunday mornings at 10:00 A.M., Buccaneer Bob casts off with a crew of pint-size pirates for a rambunctious pirate cruise of the lakefront.

Ol' Bob traces the ship's route on his pirate map, and shares a treasure chest of kidfacts about Chicago and its lakefront. While Bob works the crowd, the ship's captain presents an easy-to-understand commentary about Chicago's past and present, pointing out highlights like the museums and the lock system.

Buccaneer Bob welcomes a pint-size crew member onboard the Wacky Pirate Cruise. *Courtesy Mercury Cruiseline.*

To help your little salt blend in, dress him or her in pirate attire. (This cruise attracts lots of repeat business, and return visitors nearly always dress up.) Buccaneer Bob will help by distributing paper pirate hats and leading his pirates in rowdy singing and kazoo playing. When it's over, your junior pirate can take home the hat, the kazoo, and a certificate of survival to show friends.

The Wacky Pirate Cruise works best for kids under 9 or 10; bigger kids may find it hokey. Reservations are a must; arrange them by calling Ticketmaster at 902-1500. Tickets are $8 for adults, $5 for kids under 12, plus the service fees and taxes that come with Ticketmaster tickets. (Groups of twenty or more can deal directly with Mercury by calling 332-1368.) Tours begin at the end of June, but you can reserve your tickets as early as May 1. Just like summer vacation, Wacky Pirate Cruises come to an end on Labor Day weekend.

Wacky Pirate Cruise
Mercury Cruiseline
Michigan Avenue and Lower Wacker Drive
332-1366

For more boating fun see chapter 7, "Maritime Chicago."

How to See Chicago While Almost Standing Still

From the Sears Tower Skydeck and the John Hancock Observatory, your kids can see all of Chicago and its environs plus parts of four states—without moving more than a yard or two.

Before you visit the Sears Tower Skydeck, take a few minutes to sit on the steps at Hartford Plaza on the northwest corner of Adams Street and Wacker Drive and look up, up, up to get a sense of the immensity of this imposing monument. Although the Skydeck has its own entrance on Jackson Street, try to visit the lobby of the office building long enough to admire Alexander Calder's *The Universe*. Every part of this giant, colorful sculpture moves; kids will be fascinated by its endless twisting spiral.

Visiting the Skydeck is a multimedia experience. Waiting in line, you hear many languages (ask the kids to count how many they hear) and pass through a gallery depicting famous Chicago landmarks. After a quick and dazzling slide show, the elevator whisks you to the top in ninety seconds.

On a clear day, the view is breathtaking. Older children will enjoy finding familiar landmarks and younger kids will be astonished that you can see all the way to O'Hare Airport and across the lake. And everyone will fight over who gets to peek through the telescope, unless you bring enough quarters to keep it going ($.50 buys about a minute of gazing). Use the helpful map to find local landmarks, and see if your kids can find their house.

The Skydeck offers a great perspective on Chicago's infrastructure. At the western edge of the Loop, it's easy to show your kids how everything–the river, the expressways, and the train tracks–radiates outward to neighborhoods, suburbs, and the rest of the Midwest. You can see trains leave the stations, and watch until they disappear. (If you stroll along the river between Adams and Monroe Streets, you'll see the same trains lined up under the sidewalk on the west bank, ready to leave Union Station for Milwaukee.)

For less infrastructure and more beauty, visit the John Hancock Observatory. Your kids will see fewer trains but more boats, less grit and more grandeur, as the lakefront sweeps north from the Gold Coast toward Wisconsin. The view is especially inspiring on summer days when the lake is dotted with boats.

The Skydeck is open in winter seven days a week, 9:00 A.M. to 9:30 P.M.; in summer from 9:00 A.M. to 10:30 P.M. Call for ticket prices and seasonal hours. Hancock Observatory hours are 9:00 A.M. to midnight. Admission is $4.75 for adults, $3.75 for students 5–17, and free for kids under 5. Lines can be long at both of these popular tourist destinations. To minimize the wait, visit early in the day or after dinner on a weekday. If you visit between noon and 6:00 P.M. during the week or anytime on the weekend, the line will be long.

Sears Tower Skydeck
233 S. Wacker Drive
875-9696

John Hancock Observatory
875 N. Michigan Avenue
751-3681

2

Urban Adventures

Leave staid, deliberate sightseeing to grown-ups without kids. Treat your family to these weird, wacky, and wonderful adventures in the Big Onion.

The Subterranean Loop

There are lots of ways to see the Loop with kids, but one of the most fun is to leave the surface and go underground. Visiting subway platforms, subterranean newsstands, and the eerie depths of Lower Wacker Drive via the Loop pedway gives kids a real sense of the underside of a great city.

To navigate the pedway system as it runs in fits and starts from City Hall to the far reaches of Illinois Center, pick up the *'Round About the Loop* brochure from the Chicago Cultural Center and use its map to plot your way. Make a note of your entry and exit points, and you can marvel together at how much ground can be covered *under* ground. If you travel to the Loop by subway, you can spend a couple of hours there without ever seeing daylight!

The long tunnels of the pedway system invite all sorts of wild kid behavior, but on a busy workday (when this tour is safest and most interesting) it should be nipped in the bud. Running, screaming, and sliding around on the floor will only earn dirty looks from people who are trying to work for a living. Polite behavior can be rewarded with a treat from any of the dozens of fast-food joints, or with a detour into an office or hotel lobby (try the Hyatt Regency, where kids can marvel at the waterfalls and ponds inside the enormous atrium).

From the tunnels under Illinois Center, you can exit directly onto Lower Wacker Drive. Hold hands and peek into the gloomy netherworld of Lower Michigan Avenue, or walk across the bridge on the lower level and see the Billy Goat Tavern and the loading docks of the Sun-Times and Tribune buildings. The massive steel girders, concrete walls, and enormous loading docks will give your whole family a sense of Chicago's powerful infrastructure; the cardboard box shelters of the homeless will prompt a spirited discussion about how we should care for the city's forgotten denizens.

You can make a journey to the bottom of the Loop in any season. But keep in mind that during really cold weather, one parent will be left holding the coats and mittens. Why not try this on a really *hot* day instead, when underground tunnels make a cool retreat?

The State of Illinois Center: A Dozen Great Glass Elevators

A family visit to the State of Illinois Center, now officially called the James R. Thompson Center, lets you discourse on the bicameral legislature, answer thoughtful questions like, *What is a governor?* and *Who is our state representative?*, or share your views on the state of the state. Or you can skip the civics lesson and spend the day riding up and down the elevators.

Two banks of great glass elevators soar up eighteen floors in the stunning atrium of this controversial building. Kids will love watching the ground shrink as they rise up, up, up to the very top. For the fastest ride and the biggest thrill, take the express elevator. You can go straight up and down without having your ascent or descent interrupted by state workers traveling between floors.

With its eye-catching exterior, enormous interior, indoor waterfall, basement food court, and multiple escalators, the James R. Thompson Center is an all-round kid favorite. (It can be a highlight of the subterranean Loop tour!) Even the Dubuffet sculpture out in front inspires a hide-and-seek game. Just one word of caution: when state offices are closed, so are the elevators. You may be able to visit the lower floors of the building, but guards will prevent you from entering the elevators. Visit this one when you're guaranteed a ride.

James R. Thompson Center
100 W. Randolph Street
Reputed information number (Good luck getting an answer!): 814-6667

The Magnificent Mile

Even kids who weren't born with a silver spoon in their mouths can revel in a window-shopping trip to Michigan Avenue.

The wonders begin with the exciting view from the Michigan Avenue bridge. All those buildings and bridges, and all those people: there's something to see up, down, and every which way.

Take a short trip down the stairs in front of the Wrigley Building for a quick peek at the green-lit, eerie depths of Lower Michigan Avenue and the landmark Billy Goat Tavern. Seeing the depths adds a nice contrast to the spires around you.

Next, stop and watch the action in the WGN studio facing Michigan Avenue on the ground level of the Tribune Tower. Even when the studio is empty, kids can admire the equipment and the multicolored Chicago traffic map.

Tribune Tower itself is a lesson in geography, history, and the collector's impulse. Embedded in its walls are fragments of famous buildings, all collected and installed by Colonel McCormick, founder of the *Trib*. Finding pieces of the Great Wall of China, the Pyramids, and architectural legends on Michigan Avenue brings world history alive for young kids.

North of the Tribune Tower, the retail wonders of Michigan Avenue begin. Before you start exploring these stores, set some ground rules. Is purchasing something completely out of the question, or will you actually shop? If you shop, how much can each kid spend? Remind your kids that these stores use their flashy opulence to tempt browsers to buy–especially **Nike Town** (669 N. Michigan Avenue, 642-6363), which is simply bursting with wonders.

Check out the fluorescent-colored tropical fish in the stark white tank behind shelves of shoes, the people swimming on video screens under the floor, the transparent dumbwaiter that lifts merchandise from floor to floor, and of course, the larger-than-life posters of famous Nike endorsers.

A video paradise awaits you inside the **Sony Gallery** (663 N. Michigan Avenue, 943-3334), where big-screen televisions are stacked in huge piles and the latest in video equipment is on display for kids to try.

Crate & Barrel's merchandise is a bore for kids, but the escalator ride offers a primo view of Michigan Avenue (646 N. Michigan Avenue, 787-5900). Ditto the very grown-up **Terra Museum** (664 N. Michigan Avenue, 664-3939). On Tuesday, when admission is free, it's worth a stop to admire the second-floor view, ride the cavernous elevator (guaranteed to be the biggest your kid has ever seen), and use the bathroom.

Around the Water Tower, there are horses to admire, benches to rest on, and the Water Tower itself to contemplate. (Basically, the Water Tower is an elaborate standpipe that prevents changes in water pressure from creating a flood. It is also home to the city's Welcome Center, where you can pick up free brochures on Chicago's many attractions.) Across the street, Water Tower Place boasts a great glass elevator second only to the one in the James R. Thompson Center. Take the express up and down a couple of times before visiting a store or enjoying a meal at **foodlife** (see chapter 16, "Kid Food"). A visit to the fabulous toy emporium **F.A.O. Schwartz** will end your Michigan Avenue store crawl on a high note (840 N. Michigan Avenue, 587-5000).

When your kids need to take a break, stop by Seneca Park, right behind the Pumping Station, between Chicago Avenue and

Delaware Street. It features two cozy playgrounds: one for tots under 5, one for the big kids. For cheap snacks, visit Walgreens at Chicago and Michigan Avenues. Bathrooms are available inside Water Tower Place.

If you have time, you might consider stopping at Here's Chicago, where you can learn facts about Chicago's water system as you tour the pumping plant and enjoy a fast-paced movie and slide show that features thrilling aerial footage of the Loop and the river. This commercial monument to Chicago's past also includes a gory diorama of the St. Valentine's Day Massacre, slightly silly monuments to the Great Chicago Fire and the Great Chicago Flood, and a life-size, animated model of Abraham Lincoln, reading from his second inaugural address.

Michigan Avenue stores generally open at 10:00 A.M. and close at 8:00 P.M., closing earlier on Saturday and Sunday evenings. Here's Chicago offers continuous tours and showings from 9:30 A.M. until 5:00 P.M., staying open an hour later in the summer.

Here's Chicago
Pearson Street and Michigan Avenue
467-7114

All the Pretty Little Horses

On the 1400 block of North Orleans Street, the sights, smells and sounds of horses mix with the overhead rumble of the Ravenswood el. It's a great expedition for kids who are mad about horses!

Just west of Wells Street and south of North Avenue, this narrow street is brimming with horses, carriages, groomers, and handlers associated with two of Chicago's horse and carriage companies: Chicago Horse and Carriage and the Noble Horse. Watch your step_horse manure is everywhere, but so are gorgeous manes and gleaming hansoms and carriages.

The best time to visit the block is weekdays between 4:00 and 6:30 P.M., when carriage drivers are preparing for their evening work. By law, horse and carriage companies must be off the streets

during rush hour and cannot return to Michigan Avenue until
7:00 P.M. On weekends, shifts are continuous and crowds of horses
are harder to find.

On the street or in the yard at 1410 N. Orleans Street, your
kids will see the horses being fed and curried, and the carriages
dusted and polished. The horses are beautiful to watch, but
remember, horses can kick, so it's a good idea not to let your
children walk directly behind a horse. Ask the handler before
you pat or touch the horses.

For decades, horses have been boarded in barns like these.
Years ago, liveries housed horses and wagons used to deliver
goods, or horses and carriages for wealthy residents. Later, barns
held horses for pleasure riding in Lincoln Park. Riders started at
the south end of the park, and rode north to the Saddle & Cycle
Club at Foster Avenue, established as the terminus of a one-day
excursion in the park.

You can get a whiff of the old days inside the Noble Horse,
which still boards horses and runs the only fully equipped
equestrian center within the Chicago city limits. There's plenty
to take in. Your young horse lover can savor the aroma of hay,
horse, and leather, and watch lessons being conducted in the
200-by-75-foot indoor riding arena. She can watch confident
young riders tacking up, leading horses back to their stalls, or
returning bridles, saddles, and other riding gear to the wood-
planked walls.

If your horse lover is at least 7 years old, she can take lessons.
Prices range from $25 to $40 an hour for private lessons and $30
an hour for semiprivate lessons to $24 an hour for a group lesson.
Lessons are offered from 1:00 to 8:00 P.M.

And if she's a real horse fanatic, sign her up for the Noble
Horse's full-day summer camp, which blends creative and athletic
programs with riding lessons. Besides visiting the beach and local
museums, kids take field trips to stable facilities, the barns at
Arlington Race Track, the Tempel Farm Lippizanner stallions,
and participate in a horse show.

While girls outnumber boys, riding activities at the Noble
Horse are *not* for girls only: young boys who want to learn to
ride will find plenty of male company here!

The Noble Horse Equestrian Center
1410 N. Orleans Street
266-7878

Chicago Horse and Carriage Company
1428 N. Orleans Street
944-6773

Visit the Dead

When your family can't decide whether to enjoy an afternoon outdoors, bone up on the Civil War, or hunt for ghosts, compromise on a trip to Rosehill Cemetery.

As you enter, you'll see something familiar about the crenellated, yellow limestone castle that flanks Rosehill's gate. That's because the Rosehill facade was designed by William Boyington, who built the Water Tower six years later. Rosehill Castle and the Water Tower are the only two Boyington structures still standing in Chicago.

Rosehill Cemetery sits on 350 acres of parkland bounded by Ravenswood, Bowmanville, Western, and Peterson Avenues. Mature trees, imposing mausoleums, and twisting paths make for an atmospheric walk or drive. You can sit by one of the cemetery's five lakes and watch the antics of resident mallards, heron, and Canadian geese. (If you're driving, watch out for geese on the road.) Kids can chase squirrels, search for the foxes or the coyotes that live near Western Avenue, or wander around among the fascinating monuments on Rosehill's grounds.

To the north of the entrance, along the Chicago and North Western Railway tracks, stands an elevator once used to lower coffins from the railway embankment into the cemetery. At one time, Rosehill had a full-fledged station that matched the Boyington gateway, but the cemetery was dropped from the CNW schedule when cemetery visits ceased to be part of the social pattern.

Rosehill was chartered in 1859, just in time to receive its share of Civil War casualties. A cluster of military monuments stands

The George Bangs monument, which depicts the railway mail car designed by Bangs, is one of hundreds of unique and haunting monuments at Rosehill Cemetery. *Courtesy David Wendell.*

inside the entrance, starting with the Soldiers' Monument, a towering spire where a bugle-carrying soldier surveys his surroundings. Ringing the monument are memorials to individual fighting units and dozens of small white military gravestones marking the graves of Union soldiers who served as guards at Camp Douglas, a Civil War prison that once stood just east of where Comiskey Park is today. West of the Soldiers' Monument, members of Chicago Light Artillery Battery A are commemorated by a life-size cannon draped in a shroud.

A little north is the rock of Chickamauga, a boulder from the Georgia battlefield bearing the nickname of General George Henry Thomas, who held the field during the entire second day of the battle. Thomas is just one of the Civil War generals, captains, and majors buried in Rosehill; you can spend an afternoon just searching for and reading Civil War gravestones.

As you wander the grounds, your family will see dozens of striking memorials and hundreds of plainer gravestones. (Many are graves of children, which always fascinate kids.) One of the most interesting is the Fireman's Memorial Mound. A fire hose wraps around the base of this column, on which a mid-nineteenth-century firefighter stands proud and tall. Here are buried firefighters who have lost their lives in the line of duty in Chicago since 1864. There is space for sixty firefighters; eighteen are currently interred. Fireboxes stand at each corner of the monument and the one at the southeast end is where Kurt Russell was buried in the movie *Backdraft*.

Not to be missed are these remarkable memorials:

- The Fisher Mausoleum, a stone mausoleum disguised as an Indian burial mound

- The Taiwanese cemetery, marked by a five-foot-long granite turtle that symbolizes long life

- The George Bangs monument, a twenty-foot-tall stone oak tree under which a train car is entering a tunnel

- The Cummings cherry monument, featuring the world's largest cherry (six feet in diameter), which cost a gold prospector the fortune he made in California

Permanent residents of Rosehill include Women's Temperance Union founder Frances Willard, twelve Chicago mayors (including Levi Day Boone, Daniel's nephew), and major meat packers, manufacturers (like Ignaz Schwinn), and philanthropists.

Three celebrated residents are said to haunt the cemetery at night. Charles Hopkinson rattles chains and moans inside his mausoleum to vex plot owners who objected to his mausoleum because it would block their view. Richard Warren Sears stalks the cemetery in a top hat and tails because his retail nemesis, Aaron Montgomery Ward, is buried a mere thirty feet behind him. The quieter ghosts are Frances Pierce and her baby, who died together of tuberculosis in 1864. Look for their life-size marble sculpture behind glass, south and west of the entrance.

Another spooky stop is behind the May Memorial Chapel, alongside the cemetery's gorgeous central lake. On the hill behind the chapel are green skylights kids can peer into to see the vaults that once held bodies during the winter, when frozen ground prevented burial. It's not used anymore, but one body is left: a woman known only as "Margaret," who has lain unclaimed for more than sixty years.

To get the most out of your visit to Rosehill, stop at the office to pick up a map and a brief historical guide. The staff will give you directions to monuments of special interest to you. For very detailed information, fascinating anecdotes, and (if he's not busy) an impromptu guided tour, ask to speak to Rosehill's staff historian—especially if one of your kids is studying Civil War history. Your tour of Rosehill need not focus on death and dying. If your child is under 6, limit your visit to the lakes and emphasize open space over departed souls. Childern in elementary school, who may not entirely grasp the concept of death but find it fascinating nonetheless, will be more interested in the graves and residents. You'll be asked "How did he die?" whenever you see a child's grave.

Rosehill's Ravenswood gates are open daily from 8:30 A.M. to 5:00 P.M. Before 4:00 P.M., you can also enter through the gates on Western and Peterson Avenues. Bikes and skates are discouraged and cross-country skiing is not allowed. There is no admission fee.

Rosehill Cemetery
5800 N. Ravenswood Avenue (at Rosehill Drive)
561-5940

Hyde Park Parrots

Ah, parrots. They call up images of pirates, tropical seas, and lush, jungled islands. What a surprise to find that one flock has a Hyde Park address!

These pet store escapees live outdoors in nests that are hard to miss, especially when the trees are bare. Their massive constructions of sticks and grasses are tucked securely between the limbs of the trees. Stand underneath, and you'll see the holes the parrots use to crawl in and out of their nests.

Visiting the parrots is an all-seasons outing, because these hardy birds make it through nights when the temperature reaches twenty degrees below. It's a stupendous lesson in the adaptability of species and the survival of the fittest. Enjoy their antics at the corner of Fifty-third Street and Hyde Park Boulevard, just south of Harold's Playground, a playlot commemorating the late mayor Harold Washington, who lived nearby.

Way Out West

In the suburbs along the Eisenhower Expressway are two truly astonishing sights that will make your kids ponder what makes grown-ups tick.

Astonishing sight number one is the Elvis Shrine in Val's Halla Records (723½ South Boulevard, Oak Park, [708] 524-1004). When your kids part the beaded curtain and enter this tiny chamber, they'll be wowed by a roomful of Elvis records, plates, socks, and trading cards. As "Blue Suede Shoes" plays softly in the background, they can examine a bust of Elvis and the requisite velvet painting, and read all about recent evidence that Elvis lives. There's even a tiny fountain for making a wish.

Astonishing sight number two is a kid-pleasing monument to popular culture. Towering over Cermak Plaza at the corner of Harlem Avenue and Cermak Road is a pile of old cars impaled on a very, very tall spear, crowned by a Volkswagen bug. This is funny to behold and fascinating to decode. Ask your kids why they think it's there and what they think it means. When you've reached some conclusions, troop over to the Harlem Avenue side of the shopping center and gaze at the enormous statue of trash. It's all guaranteed to make your kids scratch their heads and wonder about the world of grown-ups.

The Southwest Side: Big Thrills

It's no secret that southsiders do things in a big way. Head for Sixty-third Street and Pulaski Road, and you'll see "big" defined in a whole new way.

A giant Indian stands atop a building that houses an eye care center, a cigar shop, and an insurance company. (Doing things in a big way doesn't have to make sense.) There are many legends about the statue's origin, but none are interesting enough to share. The giant guy is the very same Indian seen briefly in the most excellent movie, Wayne's World.

Continue driving west on Sixty-third Street and have the kiddies watch for the giant steer standing on top of a meat market. It will raise the question, "Where does hamburger actually come from?" and may even lead to a tearful yet meaningful discussion on meat consumption.

Keep driving west on Sixty-third Street and you'll find yourself at White Castle on Cicero Avenue. If your children haven't made you feel guilty about eating meat, stop and buy a sack full. If the weather permits, sit on top of the car to eat and you may be lucky enough to be directly under the path of a jet or plane landing at Midway Airport. The jets fly so low you'll think they're going to land on you. What better accompanies "sliders" than the smell of jet exhaust? Talk about a big thrill!

Don't count being this lucky with every visit, though. This flight path isn't always used. If your kids are intent on having a jet roar over their heads, try Fifty-fifth Street and Long Avenue or Fifty-ninth Street west of Cicero Avenue.

Perhaps a giant Indian and steer and going deaf under the scream of jets is not your idea of a lovely time with the children. Take a drive south along Kedzie Avenue past Eighty-seventh Street and start watching for the giant lumberjack. He stands big and strong on the roof of an auto parts shop. Mr. Lumberjack looks pretty happy, so do wave hello to him as you continue to drive down Kedzie Avenue to Ninety-second Street where you will find a unique kid's eatery called Snackville Junction (see chapter 16, "Kid Food").

If dessert is desired after all this excitement, zip around the corner to Rainbow Ice Cream at Ninety-second Street and Western Avenue. You can't miss the place. It has a giant plastic ice-cream cone on the roof!

—Peggy Zabicki
Chicago Lawn

3

Art, History, and Culture Museums
What's in Them for Kids?

Chicago's major cultural institutions are a great source of imaginative family escapades. Your kids can handle artifacts charred by the great Chicago Fire, excavate relics of an ancient city, experience the life and times of early immigrants to Chicago, and learn to draw in the shadow of the great masters—all without leaving town!

Art Institute of Chicago

Chicago's premier collection of art has plenty to offer kids. From *Nighthawks* to *A Sunday Afternoon on the Island of La Grande Jatte*, many of the masterpieces that appeal to adults also fascinate kids.

Don't miss the Impressionist Galleries, and be sure to visit Gunsalus Hall. This armory of medieval and Renaissance war tools is bursting with suits of armor, swords and scabbards, halberds, spears, and fighting axes used by knights and others who fought battles in the fifteenth and sixteenth centuries. Their finely carved handles and beautifully inlaid ivory details are a stark contrast to today's lightweight, high-tech gadgetry.

The color and detail of the paperweights in the Arthur Rubloff Paperweight Collection will also fascinate kids. Look for the paperweights with the worms and salamanders hiding inside or proudly curled on top of them.

Another surefire kid pleaser are the Thorne Miniature Rooms, conveniently located next to the Kraft General Foods Education Center. Built under the supervision of art patron Mrs. James Ward Thorne, these sixty-eight elegantly appointed rooms duplicate lavish period interiors in miniature. Each one is set in a little box that's perfect for peering into (adults have to lean down a bit, in fact, to get a good view)—and peering *through*. Each room is full of eye-stopping details—kittens playing on the hearth, a book casually left on a table, a pair of greyhounds waiting for their master—just begging to be noticed.

Kids and grown-ups alike will crane their necks to catch sight of the room's backdrop, but the illusion just keeps going, right through the windows. The South Carolina interiors open onto trees dripping with moss. Mount Fuji towers over the Japanese interior. And the Taos, New Mexico, dining room overlooks a cactus garden and commands a view of an Indian pueblo and faraway, arid peaks. Though it has no view, most splendid of all the rooms is the late thirteenth-century English Roman Catholic cathedral, set in a box far larger than the others.

The Kraft General Foods Education Center does a bang-up job of helping children look at art. Computer games that help kids learn more about the people who created various masterpieces, and what these works may mean. To draw attention to elements in a Mary Cassatt portrait of two little girls, for example, the bigger girl talks about sitting for her portrait and complains that her little sister, who ran into the picture at the last minute, always steals the show.

In the center, kids can watch an artist painting an oil or acrylic work (it's OK to ask questions!), or admire original illustrations from contemporary children's books. Don't miss *Art Inside Out*, which uses videos, signage, and hands-on activities to help kids see the meaning of a dozen items in the collection. This exhibit's strength is in helping kids grasp the beauty and significance of ceremonial items like masks, vases, pendants, and figures. Even grown-ups will enjoy seeing the details of small items that most patrons merely glance at.

You can also pick up a Family Self-Guide or a Gallery Game, which use clues and questions to involve kids in searching for various items in the Art Institute's collection, and interpreting each item's elements, technique, and meaning.

Family Programs

Every Saturday, families with kids 9 and up can enjoy a Family Gallery Walk that introduces a slice of the Art Institute's wonders. One walk might visit works of art featuring snow, another might look at Picasso's women, or lions and other elegant animals, and food and flowers in art. Gallery walks begin in Gallery 100 at 1:00 P.M. on Saturday.

If your kids are under 9, you can enjoy weekend family workshops that link a close look at art with a hands-on art experience. In both the Early Bird Workshops for kids 4 to 6 and the Family Workshops for kids 7 and over, docents lead kids and their parents on a visit to a gallery. After a stimulating discussion, the group returns to the Kraft Education Center to work on a project related to what they've seen. At Halloween, for example, the Early Bird group might look at masks in the Institute's collection, while older kids search for art portraying monsters and beasts. Early Bird programs are offered Saturday at 10:30 A.M.; Family Workshops are held Saturdays and Sundays at 2:30 P.M.

When grandparents visit, pack them off to the Grand Program, specially designed for kids over 6 and their grandparents. Together, grandparents and grandkids enjoy a special tour, activities, and a chance to share their perspectives and memories with each other. The Grand Program is held the first Sunday of the month from 12:30 to 2:00 P.M.

Imagine your child sitting down with a pencil and practicing drawing techniques under an instructor's patient gaze! That's what kids 9 and over can experience in the Drawing in the Galleries program, held the third Sunday of each month. Preregistration is required for this program and all the others described here (except the Family Gallery Walks). Sign up in the Kraft Education Center when you arrive, or call the Program Information number below for further instruction on how to register.

Logistics

The Art Institute of Chicago is open Monday, Wednesday, Thursday, and Friday from 10:30 A.M. to 4:30 P.M.; Tuesday from 10:30 A.M. to 8:00 P.M.; Saturday from 10:00 A.M. to 5:00 P.M.; and Sunday and holidays from 12:00 to 5:00 P.M. Admission is $6.50 for adults, and $3.25 for children and senior citizens. Tuesdays are free.

Reasonably priced meals are available in the Court Cafeteria, although you can also take a break from museum-watching and wander over to Wabash Avenue for a fast-food meal. Bathrooms are handicapped accessible and changing tables are available in the handicapped stall.

Art Institute of Chicago
III S. Michigan Avenue
General information: 443-3600
Program information: 443-3680
Services for the disabled: 443-3933

Balzekas Museum of Lithuanian Culture

This charming museum gives kids a chance to immerse themselves in the pageantry and weaponry of medieval Lithuania. In the interactive children's gallery, kids can try on medieval costumes, put together an oversize wooden puzzle of a knight in armor, and act out important Lithuanian battles of yore. An exhibit on nineteenth-century Lithuanian life features a large model of a thatch-roofed farmhouse and many beautiful dolls, ornaments, and instruments.

The Balzekas Museum is also an excellent source of classes in folk art skills like Easter egg coloring and ornament design.

Logistics

The Balzekas Museum is open seven days a week from 10:00 A.M. to 4:00 P.M. Admission is $4 for adults, $3 for students and seniors, and $1 for children. As for bathrooms, the Balzekas is located in a former hospital. "Practically every other room is a bathroom!" chuckled the attendant when I asked.

Balzekas Museum of Lithuanian Culture
6500 S. Pulaski Road
582-6500

Bicycle Museum of America

In this museum is absolutely the best collection of bikes your kids have ever seen! One whiff of the air in the Bicycle Museum of America, and parents will be transported back to the smells of a *real* bike store—wooden planks, rubber tires, and grease.

Formerly the corporate collection of the Schwinn Company, this marvelous collection represents a century of bicycles. It captures kids immediately with a fascinating video that tells the history of bikes from the very first bicycle—a running machine, circa 1817, propelled by feet instead of pedals—through the high-wheel cycle craze and the invention of the safety bike. A row of antique high-wheel bikes will intrigue the whole family. It just doesn't seem possible that anyone every really rode these impossibly dangerous vehicles!

But best of all is turning the corner and seeing a long, gleaming row of Schwinn bicycles from the thirties, forties, and fifties. You can sigh over the polished chrome handlebars and fenders, and the carefully crafted theme bikes like the Gene Autry Flying Westerner—a brown bicycle with a leather "saddle" and a horse's head mounted on the front—and the Hopalong Cassidy, a black and white wonder equipped with a holster.

Grandparents can point out the bikes they rode to Mickey Mouse Club matinees back in the thirties. Mom and Dad can finally show Junior what a banana seat looks like, or reminisce once more about that sturdy old paper-route bike. It's all here, and it's irresistible.

Besides the bicycles, there is a great collection of posters, artifacts, and articles that reveal the bicycle's role in women's emancipation (bloomers were invented for bike riding) and nineteenth- and twentieth-century recreation. All in all, the Bicycle Museum of America has 50,000 items, and grand plans to sponsor special bicycle-related events.

Logistics

The Bicycle Museum of America is open Monday through Friday from 10:00 A.M. to 6:00 P.M., Friday and Saturday from 10:00 A.M. to 8:00 P.M., and Sunday from noon until precisely 5:14 P.M.! Admission is $1. Handicapped-accessible bathrooms are located outside the museum in the North Pier complex.

Bicycle Museum of America
North Pier Festival Market
435 E. Illinois Street
222-0500

Camp Douglas Museum

During the Civil War, a Union prison camp stood just east of the site of today's Comiskey Park. Your family can still find traces of Civil War history in the Griffin Funeral Home, where Captain Ernie Griffin has created a small museum honoring soldiers who served in the war.

Mr. Griffin's grandfather, private Charles H. Griffin, trained for the Civil War at Camp Douglas after enlisting in the Twenty-ninth Illinois Infantry, the first African American unit dispatched from Illinois. To commemorate his grandfather and others who served, Mr. Griffin's museum displays a saber used by a soldier in the unit—one of the few artifacts of this regiment on display in the state. Other items in his collection include a Springfield rifle, standard issue to Union soldiers, a cavalry bugle, a pair of replica cannons used by the artillery of both sides, and pictures of the camp in its heyday.

In the parking lot outside the funeral home, Mr. Griffin has erected a Heritage Memorial Wall displaying miniature flags of the Confederate and Union states. Nearby is a plaque commemorating the 6,000 Confederate soldiers who died at Camp Douglas—many by freezing to death in thin tents that provided little shelter from the bitter winter weather. Also erected by Mr. Griffin, it is the city's only monument to this vanished piece of history.

The museum is located in the south portico of Griffin Funeral Home, open Monday through Friday from 8:30 A.M. to 5:00 P.M., and there is no admission charge for viewing the Civil War exhibit. However, to make sure your visit doesn't interrupt a funeral or a wake, call before you visit. Griffin Funeral Home recommends that you call a day ahead to make sure Mr. Griffin will be on the premises and available to take you through his display. Call and confirm your plans on the morning of your visit.

Camp Douglas Museum
3232 S. Martin Luther King Drive
842-3232

Chicago Historical Society

The Chicago Historical Society is an absolute must for any child who is just beginning to study Chicago, Illinois, and U.S. history. On any given day, its halls are crowded with parents and children researching papers on Jean Baptiste Point DuSable, the Chicago Fire, and other notable people and events.

On the first floor are two great galleries for kids. The Hands-On History Gallery lets kids handle artifacts rescued from the Chicago Fire, play with nineteenth-century toys, compare old and new views of State Street, and learn more about the fur trade that led settlers to this area. In the adjoining Pioneer Life Gallery, early maps and paintings of Illinois territory are accompanied by model rooms from a pioneer home, a blacksmith shop, a school, and a printing house. Sometimes the rooms are staffed by volunteers who demonstrate printing, candle making, spinning, weaving, and quilt making, and show how farm implements were used.

Tucked into the rear of the first floor is the Fort Dearborn Gallery, where a wall resembling the original Fort Dearborn contains timber rescued from the *second* Fort Dearborn. (If you didn't know there were two, head here first!)

The Chicago History Gallery on the second floor is bursting with artifacts from "the old days." (Some of them are of rather recent vintage, like the courtesy cup from the original Des Plaines McDonald's!) Older children will be interested in the stories behind the artifacts, like the sad letter from a woman to Mayor Dever asking him to close the "blind pig" bar where her husband drank every night.

Kids will be gripped by the eleven-minute laser disc on the Chicago Fire, which gives a sense of the fire's devastating effect on Chicago families, as well as its influence on the city's appearance today. Also favored by kids are the Chicago dioramas, scale models that depict Chicago as a fur-trading outpost, a growing city, a city in flames, and a city of prosperity.

Preteens and teenagers will enjoy the Civil War Gallery, which presents the view that slavery was at the war's root. The exhibit shows how slaves were marketed, as well as how abolitionists and others (including many Chicago residents) resisted the slave trade. Visitors can listen to a four-minute excerpt from the famous Lincoln-Douglas debates on slavery. And everyone who visits is amazed to find President Lincoln's deathbed–the real thing!–in this display.

Family Programs

On the second Saturday of each month between noon and 2:00 P.M., CHS offers Kidstory, an informal program that gives children and adults new ways to relate to history in their lives. Craft activities encourage kids to take a fresh, creative look at the past and present. A typical Saturday may include games from the past and present, an oral history workshop that teaches kids how to capture their own family history, or a chance to make and wear an architectural hat of the city.

Logistics

The Chicago Historical Society is open Monday through Saturday from 9:30 A.M. to 4:30 P.M., and Sunday from noon to 5:00 P.M. Admission is $3 for adults, $3 for seniors and students with valid school ID, and $1 for children 6–17. There is no admission charge on Monday.

The Hands-On History Gallery is open Monday through Friday from noon to 2:00 P.M., Saturday from 11:00 A.M. to 4:30 P.M., and Sunday from noon to 4:30 P.M.

Bathrooms are located on the first floor near the coat check, where you can also leave strollers, diaper bags, and other paraphernalia.

Chicago Historical Society
Clark Street at North Avenue
642-4600

The DuSable Museum of African American History

The best way for a child to view this collection, dedicated to educating the public about African American history, art, and culture, is to visit it during a field trip. But your family can enjoy the museum by calling ahead to arrange a ninety-minute lecture, a film, and a tour of museum highlights. It imparts a wealth of information about African and African American history and great African American achievers. Tours are offered daily between 10:00 A.M. and 1:00 P.M., but you must preregister to participate.

In 1995, the museum opened a hands-on Children's Discovery Gallery designed to teach young children about Africa and its impact on the New World. Call for more information about the gallery and its activities.

Family Programs

On Saturday, the DuSable Museum often shows videos on different African cultures and invites storytellers to interpret African folktales. Call the museum for a schedule of these special family events.

Logistics

The DuSable Museum is open Monday through Saturday from 10:00 A.M. to 4:00 P.M., and Sunday from noon to 4:00 P.M. Admission is $3 for adults, $2 for students, and $1 for children 6–13.

DuSable Museum of African American History
740 E. Fifty-sixth Place
947-0600

Mexican Fine Arts Center Museum

This marvelous museum offers ambitious arts programming year round. From summertime art classes for neighborhood kids to the winter celebration of Mexican Women Writers, its calendar is filled with exciting celebrations of Mexican art and culture.

But the best time to visit the Mexican Fine Arts Museum is during October, when it mounts its annual *Dia de los Muertes* exhibit. In Mexico, All Souls Day (November 2) is regarded as a day when the souls of the departed return home to join their families. To entice them, families set up *ofrendas* or altars filled with the deceased's favorite food and drink, plus items of clothing, family pictures, tools, and favorite objects used by the deceased. The altar becomes a bridge between two worlds, helping the soul to join its family, and creating a feeling that the deceased is present.

During October, the museum displays typical ofrendas along with the arts and crafts items used to celebrate this day: all of them skeletons. You'll see nearly life-size skeletons dressed in the costumes of organ grinders, knife sharpeners, bakers, doctors, and bicycle delivery men. There are skeletons made from clay, metal, paper, and sugar, all surrounded by dazzling colors and shapes. An excellent video explains the origins of the Dia de los Muertes and the customs that celebrate it.

The museum is free, so bring a little extra cash to spend in its wonderful gift shop. Let your kids buy inexpensive candy skulls made of sugar–a real dentist pleaser–or clay skulls of varying sizes, some with string-operated jaws that open and close.

Logistics

The Mexican Fine Arts Museum is open Tuesday through Sunday from 10:00 A.M. to 4:45 P.M. Admission is free. Don't worry about the big sign saying no public bathrooms; that is directed to passersby and patrons of the park. There are bathrooms inside for your family.

Finding the museum can be tricky. On the Southwest Side, numbered streets alternate with numbered places; you want Nineteenth *Street*, not Nineteenth Place.

After you visit the museum, go around the corner to Eighteenth Street (not Place!) and enjoy a taco at one of the many taquerias in Pilsen's commercial district. With three dining rooms, **Nuevo Leon** (1515 W. Eighteenth Street, 421-1517) is one of the biggest and friendliest, but almost any taqueria can feed your family delicious tacos and sodas for a very modest price.

Mexican Fine Arts Center Museum
1852 W. Nineteenth Street
738-1503

Museum of Broadcast Communications

Wanna take a screen test? You and your family can at the Museum of Broadcast Communications' Kraft Television Center, where you can produce your own TV news show.

Up to four people can don gold blazers and read the news from teleprompters as the staff films your segment. (Kids do have to be able to read to participate.) This is a blast to do and even more fun later, when you see yourselves looking oh-so-serious in front of the station logo! For $19.95, you'll have twenty minutes of footage you'll treasure forever. This is a great gift for grandparents, and a great way to capture a grandparent on film.

On Saturday morning, the museum also screens *OllieFest*, which showcases past winners of the Ollie award for excellent children's programming. Winners of Europe's Prix Jeunesse are also shown. Choose this as an alternative to Saturday morning cartoons, and your kids can watch award-winning programs from around the world like the British TV series *The Borrowers*, based on the books by Mary Norton.

Pining for Annette Funicello or Garfield Goose? You can show your child a favorite TV show from your youth by visiting the museum's public archives. Just look up the program, complete a request card, and your family can watch it in one of the twenty-six screening carrels on the premises. The archives contain 49,000 hours of radio programs, 6,000 TV programs, and 8,000 TV commercials.

For kids writing civics and history papers, these archives are an invaluable source of original broadcasts of presidential debates, broadcast news, and documentaries, including thirty hours alone of broadcasts on President Kennedy.

Logistics

The Museum of Broadcast Communications is located in the landmark Chicago Cultural Center. It is open Monday through Saturday from 10:00 A.M. to 4:30 P.M.; Sunday from noon to 5:00 P.M.

Museum of Broadcast Communications
Michigan Avenue at Washington Street
629-6000
To film a TV news segment of your family, call 629-6010.

Oriental Institute

To kids, archeological artifacts and ancient Near East history can seem dry as dust—unless they visit the Oriental Institute at the University of Chicago on Sunday afternoon.

Every Sunday during the school year, families can drop by between 12:30 and 3:30 P.M. for a short, guided tour and a quick, kid-oriented project that both relate to an overall theme. The themes, which change monthly, provide a helpful lens through which kids learn to understand a very intricate period of history.

What will kids do? When the focus is on ancient Egypt, kids can write their names in hieroglyphics, make jewelry for a princess or a pharaoh, or make an Egyptian mask. To learn more about Mesopotamia, kids make and write messages on clay tablets. During February, when the museum celebrates African American history month, kids enjoy fun and games from the ancient culture of Nubia. On any given Sunday, your family might make clay pots, bracelets and pendants, Egyptians toys, or a crown for your family's own "Queen Mom."

Don't worry if you're not there precisely at 12:30. Several tours depart during the Family Program, and the craft activity is ongoing. If you arrive between tours, your kids can make the craft first, and take the tour later. There's also a movie to watch at 2:00 P.M. While all the topics sound appealing—Egyptian pyramids, a day in the life of a pharaoh, and so on—some of the movies talk right over kids' heads. Ask the Family Program leader if the movie being shown during your visit is one your family will enjoy.

No reservations are needed for Sunday Family Programs. All activities are free, as is the museum.

A Sunday Family Workshop is the best way to introduce your family to this museum, which can be very hard to appreciate without a guide. But if you do visit the Oriental Institute on your own, pick up one the museum's Treasure Hunt maps. By following twenty-five clues, kids can locate and learn more about twenty-five different objects in the collection.

A fabulous way to grasp the Oriental Institute is to combine it with a visit to the Spertus Museum of Judaica, where kids can excavate items from an archeological "tell" (a mound of remains from ancient settlements) of the same historical era: 3,500 to 700 B.C. Your kids can see the real artifacts at the Oriental Institute, and then dig for replicas in the sand at Spertus!

Family Programs

To make its arcane collection more accessible, the Oriental Institute often collaborates with other institutions. With the Lincoln Park Zoo, it has developed Ancient Animals, a field trip that begins by visiting the animals tamed, hunted, and worshipped in ancient Egypt, Sumeria, and Persia, and ends in the Oriental Institute, where families see how ancient civilizations portrayed these creatures and kids make their own ancient animal toy.

The Oriental Institute also works closely with the Smart Museum of Art, particularly during the annual June Family Day, when the two museums sponsor a day of performances and activities that highlight their collections.

Besides Sunday Family Programs, the Oriental Institute offers special kids-only tours of the gallery during the summer. These Thursday morning tours let 6- to 12-year-olds get a privileged look inside the museum, and enjoy an activity centered on the objects they view. Call the museum's Education Department for information on these tours and field trips.

Logistics

The Oriental Institute at the University of Chicago is open Tuesday, Thursday, Friday, and Saturday from 10:00 A.M. to 4:00 P.M., Wednesday from 10:00 A.M. to 8:30 P.M., and Sunday from noon to 4:00 P.M. Admission is free.

In 1996 the Oriental Institute is scheduled to be renovated. Programming may be interrupted by the renovation, so call before you go to make sure the Sunday Family Programs are proceeding as planned.

Oriental Institute at the University of Chicago
1155 E. Fifty-eighth Street
General information: 702-9521
Education and public programs: 702-9507

Spertus Museum of Judaica

This very grown-up collection of very serious artifacts boasts one amazing children's attraction: the Rosenbaum Children's ARTiFACT Center.

This replica of an archeological dig site brings ancient Middle Eastern history alive by teaching children about the tools, practices, and purposes of archaeology. Before they begin, kids get an earful on the digging process and their responsibilities at the dig site, which include putting everything they find back and cleaning up any spilled sand. Once prepared, they are set loose in the ten-foot-tall, thirty-two-foot-long tell, an imaginary dig site whose artifacts cover 1,500 years of history—from the time of Pharaoh Ramses II to the year A.D. 200.

Buried in the tell are jugs, decanters, oil lamps, jewelry, statuettes, household items, tools, weapons, helmets, and dozens of other items. As kids dig, they log their discoveries in field notebooks. When they have finished, they can discover the age and the history of each artifact they have collected. Parents are encouraged to participate, and few can resist!

The thirty-two-foot-long tell is surrounded by an ancient marketplace where learning stations reveal how people lived in the ancient world. One station uses rubber stamps to demonstrate ancient scripts, another offers a trade and travel game that teaches kids about what kinds of goods were valued and the ancient trade routes they followed. For a real taste of life in ancient times, kids can play with clay in the pottery booth, make amulets, paper sandals, and try on costumes typical of the era.

The tell was designed with junior high schoolers in mind, but younger children can be accommodated if they want to know more about ancient civilizations. But if your children are so young that all they see is an elaborate sandbox, wait a few years for your visit, or direct them to the Israelite House, a model of a 3,000-year-old Israeli home where they can act out family life.

For a real "a ha!" experience, couple your visit to the Rosenbaum Children's ARTiFACT Center with a visit to the Oriental Institute of the University of Chicago. Once kids have dug up replicas from the tell, they will enjoy discovering the real thing in the Oriental Institute.

Family Programs

Every Sunday, a video camera is set up in the marketplace area so kids can see themselves on camera when they are dressed in ancient finery. Arts workshops are often scheduled on Sunday afternoons. A typical workshop may involve making replicas of ancient pottery and oil lamps, creating a clay tablet for writing, or making jewelry. Puppet shows based on Hebrew folktales are offered quarterly on Sundays at 2:00 P.M. Call the museum to find out when the next workshop or puppet show is offered.

Logistics

Children who want to dig in the tell will be most comfortable wearing gym shoes and long pants. According to the staff, the tell is never uncomfortably crowded except during the spring school vacation, when you might want to visit early. The museum provides plenty of space for coats and gear, and bathrooms are nearby. The ARTiFACT Center is open Sunday through Thursday from 1:00 to 4:30 P.M. Admission is $4 for adults, and $2 for students, children, and seniors. (The $9 family rate is a great deal for families with three or more members.)

Secure parking is available at a nearby city-owned lot or in the Hilton Hotel.

Spertus Museum of Judaica
Rosenbaum ARTiFACT Center
618 S. Michigan Avenue
ARTiFACT Center line: 322-1754

Swedish American Museum

This cozy museum in the Andersonville neighborhood documents the migration of Swedes to Chicago, whose Swedish population at one time exceeded Stockholm's.

The Swedish immigration experience is imaginatively presented in the children's exhibit, *From Vikings to Volvs*, dominated by an enormous Viking ship that kids can climb on, wearing typical Viking clothing and fierce Viking helmets. While they're dressed as Vikings, have the kids write their names in runic characters, and unscramble a runic message.

There is more dress up fun in the traditional Swedish log cabin, where kids can wear old Swedish clothing and try out the straw mattress. If the life of a Swedish bondsman is not for them, they can pack a trunk, figure out how long they'll have to work to buy a ticket to America, and board the immigrant ship, where they can experience firsthand the dark, cramped quarters people endured during the long voyage overseas.

The exhibit also highlights the achievements of prominent Swedish Americans like Charles Lindbergh and astronaut Buzz Aldrin. An activity center is filled with Brio toys and blocks of empty juice boxes (a Swedish invention, natch!), and kids can rest in the reading corner, stocked with Swedish and English storybooks like *Pippi Longstocking* and *The Wonderful Adventures of Nils*.

A visit to the museum is a great way to cap off a day in Andersonville. Start with a stack of delicious Swedish pancakes at the charming **Svea Restaurant** (5236 N. Clark Street, 275-7738), and be sure to visit the extensive children's book section at **Women & Children First** (5233 N. Clark Street, 769-9299).

Family Programs

Highlights of the Swedish American Museum's children's schedule are Viking Day, celebrated in October, and Santa Lucia Day, celebrated December 13. (For details, see chapter 17, "Powwows, Parties, and Parades.")

Logistics

The Swedish American Museum is open Tuesday through Friday from 10:00 A.M. to 4:00 P.M., Saturday and Sunday from 10:00 A.M. to 3:00 P.M. During December, hours are slightly extended. Admission is $2 adults, $1 for students and senior citizens; children under 12 pay $.50.

Swedish American Museum Center
5211 N. Clark Street
728-8111

4

Science, Nature, and Natural History Museums
Where Wonders Never Cease

Armed only with a few museum tickets, your children can see the stars, explore the ocean floor, learn the secrets of flight, and marvel at the way life on Earth has changed since the decline of the dinosaurs.

Adler Planetarium

With its marvelous sky show, lots of space equipment to play with and telescopes to peek through, the Adler Planetarium goes to great lengths to reveal the wonders of the galaxy to Chicago children.

On the first floor, kids can examine real space suits, model rockets, and space capsules. A real hit are the Space Transporters that introduce the terrain and gravity of Mars, the Moon, Jupiter, and the Sun. When kids stand inside the transporters, they are "beamed up" to a new planet, where they discover how much they weigh in its atmosphere.

A young visitor to the planetarium uses an astrolabe mock-up to sight a distant simulated star. *Courtesy the Adler Planetarium.*

Upstairs, a display on telescopes and navigation is highlighted by a station that lets kids practice sighting stars and planets through a telescope. Kids can get an eyeful of the huge Dearborn telescope, once the largest in the world.

Everything inside the planetarium is interesting, but the sky show is the most fun. The sky show takes place in two theaters that are connected by the Stairway to the Stars, a special effects filled escalator that surrounds your family with stars that seem to go on and on forever.

Sky shows change periodically to highlight new knowledge about the heavens. While the shows are interesting to adults, young children may grow impatient with their length and detail. You can solve this problem by taking kids under 7 to one of the children's sky shows, like *The Littlest Dinosaur in Space*, shown Saturday and Sunday at 10:00 A.M.

On Friday night following the 8:00 P.M. sky show, audiences in the Sky Theater can view live pictures from outer space taken from the planetarium's Doane Observatory. Older kids who like astronomy will be intrigued by these pictures of objects millions of light-years away!

During solar eclipses, comet showers, and other special events of the heavens, helpful astronomers update visitors on activities in outer space and use the Internet to show recent satellite photos of the phenomenon. Occasionally telescopes are also set up outside the planetarium for firsthand observation of the stars.

Logistics

The planetarium is handicapped accessible and has a full-service cafeteria, Food for Thought.

A fringe benefit of a visit to the planetarium is the view. From its promontory point on Lake Michigan, there's an imposing view of the Loop, Hyde Park, the steel mills, and Indiana. Take your family for a stroll along the sidewalk that surrounds the planetarium (Hang on to little ones; the water's deep.), and consider catching a Shoreline cruise from the dock next door to the planetarium.

The Adler Planetarium is open Saturday through Thursday from 9:00 A.M. to 5:00 P.M., and Friday from 9:00 A.M. to 9:00 P.M. Admission is $4 for adults and $2 for seniors and children 4–17. The planetarium is free on Tuesdays.

Adler Planetarium
1300 S. Lake Shore Drive
322-0304

Chicago Academy of Sciences

At the Chicago Academy of Sciences, the natural history of the Midwest gets center stage. All of its exhibits promote scientific literacy and teach children about issues that affect our environment.

However, in June 1995 the Academy turned over its beloved Laflin Building to the Lincoln Park Zoological Society, which will use the former museum as office space. Until the Academy's new museum is complete in 1996, its programs and exhibits will be gypsies, setting up wherever they find shelter! During its "road trip," you can call its hotline number to find out where Academy Activities will take place.

In the summer of 1996, a new Chicago Academy of Sciences will open at Fullerton Avenue and Cannon Drive. Twice as large as the old museum, the new space will open onto Lincoln Park's North Pond, the site of exciting outdoor programs.

Inside the new Academy, you will find the dioramas of Illinois habitats and the 300-million-year-old coal forest that once greeted visitors in the old building. The refurbished dioramas will make it easier for kids to learn about prairie, sand dunes, limestone canyons, caves, and other regional habitats. Left behind in the Laflin Building, sadly, is the Atwood Celestial Sphere, the first revolving planetarium in the United States.

The new Academy building will offer an expanded Children's Gallery, where 5- to 10-year-old kids can feel antlers, meet snakes and turtles, hear nature stories, and play computer nature games. And because each exhibit will incorporate children's activities, the new Academy will be one enormous Children's Gallery!

Family Programs

The Academy offers many workshops and classes for kids, like the imaginative Knee High Naturalists programs, which use stories, demonstrations, games, and crafts to introduce 4 and 5 year olds to bats, snakes, owls, and other denizens of the natural world. During its year on the road, the Academy will continue to offer fantastic field trips to anyone 15 and over. With your teenager, you can travel to see bald eagles along the Mississippi River, or visit grasslands, dunes, and prairies in the area.

In the summer, the Academy's wonderful Science Camps teach scientific principles to kids from preschool through the third grade. Preschoolers and kindergartners can study bugs and fossils, and older kids dissect owl pellets, uncover the secrets of pond life, or go spelunking. Register in April or May for these one-week courses, which fill up quickly!

Logistics

During 1995 and the first part of 1996, the Chicago Academy of Sciences will be homeless. For hours, prices, and the location of its exhibits, call the hotline below. The same number will be used after the Academy moves in to its new Fullerton Avenue and Cannon Drive facilities in 1996.

Chicago Academy of Sciences
Education registrar: 549-0775
Information hotline: 871-2668

Dearborn Observatory

If your kid wants to see *real* stars, visit the Dearborn Observatory on the Northwestern University Campus. From April through October, the observatory opens to the public every Friday night at 9:00 P.M. On the third floor, a telescope is set up and graduate astronomy students are on hand to point out whatever is of astronomical interest that night. The eighteen-inch refracting telescope itself is of interest, since it is 100 years old.

This is a very open-ended visit; your family can stay for up to an hour, or leave when everyone has enough of peering through the telescope.

Logistics

The Dearborn Observatory can be visited by reservation only. Call to get your family's name on the Friday night list. The Dearborn Observatory is on the Northwestern University Campus just north of the Garrett Theological Seminary. Park in the big parking lot south of the seminary, and walk north along the Garrett Building to the observatory. The telescope is on the third floor.

The big white observatory on the lakefront is the Lindheimer Astronomical Research Center, closed for renovation in 1995. When you call to arrange a visit, ask whether the Lindheimer Center has reopened and is part of the tour.

**Dearborn Observatory and Lindheimer
Astronomical Research Center**
Northwestern University
Department of Physics and Astronomy
2131 Sheridan Road
Evanston
(708) 491-7650

Field Museum of Natural History

The Field Museum is home to enormous dinosaurs, lovingly detailed dioramas of midwestern habitats, an African village, and a Native American lodge, plus everything from the world's largest blue jeans to an ancient Egyptian burial chamber.

The Field Museum teaches children about the world and its people—as well as its prehistoric residents! Much too big for a single visit, the Field makes a great annual destination. No matter how your children's interests evolve, there's an exhibit to match them!

The Field Museum's most spectacular exhibit is *DNA to Dinosaurs*, which explores the history and evolution of life on Earth from the first appearance of single-celled life with DNA material 3.5 billion years ago through the age of the dinosaurs. In fact, half of the exhibit is given over to the museum's impressive collection of dinosaurs.

The second half of the story of life on Earth is told in *Teeth, Tusks & Tar Pits*, which features later giants like mammoths and saber-tooth tigers and covers topics like the Ice Age and fossilization. The exhibit is divided into three "slices of time" that focus on landmark periods and events in Earth's history. Laboratory exploration areas and the humorous "Evolutionary Broadcasting System" newscast with Bill Kurtis lets kids understand biological and geological change. Another fun display is the fantasy dentist's office, where mammals of all sizes and ages are served!

When your kids are tired of dinosaurs, they can explore the people of Africa, the Pacific, ancient Egypt, and the Americas in hall after hall of imaginative interactive displays. Children who are fascinated with Native Americans will marvel at the costumes, masks, and totem poles, and enjoy peering into the Pawnee Earth Lodge. The newly restored Maori Meeting House brings kids into contact with the culture of the Aborigines of New Zealand.

For very young children, the Place for Wonder lets kids peek inside boxes full of minerals, furs, shells, even prehistoric cockroaches! This two-room gallery is staffed by volunteers who know just how to help children get their hands on the natural world.

Family Programs

At the Field Museum, something exciting is scheduled every weekend, whether it's a dinosaur craft workshop or a performance by an African dance troupe in Stanley Field Hall. Many programs are open to anyone who wanders in, others require preregistration.

In the "wander in" category are great activities like Shell ID Day, when children can bring in their shells, snails, slugs, and other invertebrates for identification and classification. Geography games related to Africa, stories and songs from around the world, and activities with a Native American theme are all free to the public.

Formal classes and workshops are offered weekends and evenings to members and the general public. Costs range from $7 to $25 a participant, depending on whether the workshop entails a field trip. For 3- to 5-year-old children and their parents, there are Saturday workshops that let kids discover the natural world through their senses. By pretending to be dinosaurs, kids see how body parts help a dinosaur find food and defend itself. By creating simple instruments and listening to animal sounds, kids hear how the sounds of animals in the wild combine to make a music of their own. Workshops for families with school-age kids add a dollop of pedagogy to a morning of fun. A Bucket of Dinos to Go treats families to a luncheon of fried chicken and lemonade—and then has kids compare the chicken bones to fossilized dinosaur bones to see why birds are really dinosaurs in disguise!

During Field Family Evenings, the museum lets you visit the laboratories generally off-limits to visitors and banishes forever the misguided notion that they are filled with dusty, forgotten specimens. An evening in the Division of Mammals, for example, lets families see how specimens come to the museum and are measured, prepared, and cataloged for scientific study in the "prep lab." Your kids also get a close look at resident rodent and bat specimens and a visit to the Beetle Room.

Your best source for information about the Field Museum's family programs is *Field Guide*. Published three times a year by the Division of Adult, Family and Children's Programs (part of the museum's Education Department), it lists all family field trips, workshops, performances, and overnights, plus toddler and child workshops. Call 322-8854 to get on the guide's mailing list.

Logistics

The Field Museum does a great job of making families feel at home. There are child-accessible bathrooms on every floor, and a wealth of dining possibilities in the basement. The Picnic in the Field deli offers upscale sandwiches and juice. The efficient McDonald's branch dishes up Happy Meals in record time, even when the museum is mobbed during the winter school break. (Finding a table during winter vacation is next to impossible, though.)

The museum is accessible to the handicapped. Strollers and wheelchairs are available.

The Field Museum is open from 9:00 A.M. to 5:00 P.M. daily except on Thanksgiving, Christmas, and New Year's Day. Admission to the museum is $5 for adults, $3 for children, students, and seniors. Maximum general admission for families (parents and children) is $16. Admission is free on Wednesdays.

Admission to the two *Life Over Time* exhibits, *DNA to Dinosaurs* and *Teeth, Tusks & Tar Pits*, is $2 for adults and $1 for children with general admission. Tickets are subject to availability. You can purchase them in advance by calling Ticketmaster at 902-1500.

Field Museum of Natural History
Roosevelt Road at Lake Shore Drive
Adult and family programs and classes: 322-8854
General information: 922-9410

Museum of Holography

The Museum of Holography endeavors to educate the public about the process of recording images in three dimensions. School and group tours get to hear a bit about the basic physics of light and the process of using lasers to make a hologram. You can hear this, too, when a docent is available, by adding $1 to your admission fee.

Otherwise, this is a self-guided tour. The museum is small, but bursting with colorful, astonishing, and sometimes downright eerie holographic images. Walk quickly by them once to experience the sense of ever-changing rectangles of color and light. Then slow down and examine each one carefully. Eeriest of all are the portraits. It's hard not to think that those silent, still people are trapped somewhere behind the wall!

Kids will enjoy flashy holograms like the enormous Tyrannosaurus rex who juts out of its frame into the room, the microscope they can really look through, or the miner panning for gold. The scientific holograms provide fascinating pictures of the ventricles of the brain, the bones of the middle ear, and other images most of us have seen only in two dimensions.

The museum has many inexpensive holograms for sale. Perhaps its best items are the holographic diffraction gradings glasses, which let the viewer watch light bounce off surfaces. Try on a pair and watch the little holographic disks called dazers spin around and around. Even kids who think they've seen it all will find this a new experience!

Logistics

The Museum of Holography is open Wednesday through Sunday from 12:30 to 5:00 P.M. Admission is $2.50 (plus an extra $1 for the services of a docent, if you so desire). There is ample parking on the street in front of the museum.

Museum of Holography
1134 W. Washington Boulevard
226-1007

Museum of Science and Industry

It would take a lifetime to experience every hands-on exhibit in this enormous museum. One or two visits a year will introduce your family to hundreds of basic and advanced scientific concepts, from the principles of solar energy to the inner workings of the human circulation system. Here are some of the highlights.

The Coal Mine. Carved out of the ground in southern Illinois and reinstalled here in Chicago, this amazing exhibit demonstrates the dangerous conditions and hard labor associated with downstate coal mining. Giant, noisy earth-moving equipment–taken apart, moved, and reassembled underground by engineers–demonstrates how coal is blasted, scraped, and then hauled away by coal hoppers. A real explosion comes at the end of the tour, when your kids see and hear a (carefully controlled) methane gas explosion.

The long elevator descent, the underground train ride, the noisy machinery, and the eerie caves and tunnels will thrill older kids. But if your child is young enough to still fear the dark, this exhibit may be too intense.

The Railway Gallery. Big trains to steer, little trains to watch–the Railway Gallery's collection offers something for every train lover. The 3,000-square-foot Santa Fe model railroad layout lovingly portrays the landscape of New Mexico–including Native American pueblos, working oil derricks, and an adobe tourist motel atop a mesa. Kids can watch the trains from an elevated platform or from anywhere along its sides. They can also get an eyeful of several powerful locomotives and see exactly how steam engines make a locomotive's wheels turn.

Take Flight. This exhibit teaches the principles of flight through unique, multimedia computer games and an exclusive peek inside a Boeing 737 and other flying machines. Parents will be intrigued by a World War II live radio broadcast of an air battle between Allied and German fighter planes.

U-505 Submarine. A guided tour through an actual German submarine captured during World War II is followed by a film about its 1944 capture. Caution: expect long lines during school vacations.

Whispering Gallery. A child standing at one end of this hall can hear a whisper from the other end!

The Curiosity Place. Great for kids under 6. Touchable objects like musical instruments and a water table involve little ones in learning fundamental scientific principles. Another surefire winner for the small set is the Fairy Castle.

The Henry Crown Space Center and the Omnimax Theater. Among other spacecraft, the Space Center exhibits the Apollo 8 spacecraft that orbited the Moon in 1968, and the lunar module on which its astronauts trained, a replica of the first Sputnik spacecraft, and many other artifacts that illuminate the space race.

The Omnimax Theater's five-story-high screen literally surrounds viewers with dazzling images that are much larger than life. The images are so mesmerizing that one little boy at a screening of *Beavers* whispered to his father, "Dad, why aren't we wet?"

The Omnimax Theater makes any movie look good, but movies with flight sequences are particularly dizzying. Shots taken by space shuttle crews really make you feel like you're in space. All in all, an Omnimax movie is a way cool experience for children and grown-ups alike. (The current feature is shown in Spanish on Sunday at 5:30 P.M.)

Besides these highlights, the museum displays dozens of old cars, fire trucks, horse-drawn carriages, a fascinating view of the stages of the developing human embryo, an enormous walk-through human heart, and many, many more exhibits. Don't let elementary-age kids overlook the Grainger Hall of Basic Science, where scientific phenomenon are memorably demonstrated.

Logistics

Food is available in Finnigan's Ice Cream Parlor, Pizza Hut, the Century Room, the Snack Spot, and the Astro Cafe. Vending machines can be found in the Miner's Stop, at the exit of the *Coal Mine* exhibit.

Bathrooms with changing stations are available on the ground-floor opposite the Century Room dining area. There are also bathrooms adjacent to the Omnimax Theater in the Henry Crown Space Center.

Between Labor Day and Memorial Day, the museum is open Monday through Friday from 9:30 A.M. to 4:00 P.M., and Saturday, Sunday, and holidays from 9:30 A.M. to 5:30 P.M. Between Memorial Day and Labor Day, the museum is open daily from 9:30 A.M. to 5:30 P.M.

Admission to the museum is $6 for adults and $4 for children. Museum admission plus a ticket to an Omnimax show is $10 for adults and $5.50 for children. On Thursday when the museum is free, Omnimax admission alone is $6 for adults and $4 for children.

Museum of Science and Industry
Fifty-seventh Street and Lake Shore Drive
General number: 684-1414

John G. Shedd Aquarium

Spending a day in the Shedd Aquarium is the closest thing to spending a day underwater—without all that complicated diving equipment!

The aquarium's many galleries bring kids face to face with marine residents from around the world. But while plenty of sharks, whales, and electric eels live here, not all the residents are exotic. A good portion of the aquarium is devoted to freshwater fish and animals, including residents of the Great Lakes region.

Besides the high-profile oceanarium, which replicates northwestern coastal habitats, the aquarium has six galleries that display animals from warm and cold fresh waters and oceans.

All in all, 6,000 aquatic animals live in the Shedd Aquarium. Highlights include flashlight fish, visible only as tiny, darting, blinking lights; gorgeous sea anemones; an enormous alligator snapping turtle; and starving piranhas that can shred small prey to their bones in mere minutes.

These galleries surround the *Coral Reef* exhibit, where kids can watch divers hand-feeding tropical fishes at 11:00 A.M. and 2:00 P.M. on weekdays, 11:00 A.M., 2:00 P.M., and 3:00 P.M. Saturday and Sunday, and daily during the summer.

The star of the aquarium is its oceanarium, home to beluga whales, pacific white-sided dolphins, sea otters, and many other marine animals native to the Pacific Northwest. Inside the oceanarium, you can follow a nature trail that models areas of the northwest coastal habitat. At 10:30 A.M., 12:00 P.M., 1:30 P.M., 3:00 P.M., and 4:30 P.M., the Marine Mammal Presentation introduces your children to the whales and dolphins who live here. After watching the show from the amphitheater, you can wander down to the Underwater Viewing Gallery to see the same creatures from below.

Family Programs

The Special Exhibit Gallery adjoining the oceanarium is home to ever-changing special events that are free with your admission to the aquarium. During the winter, families can learn more about polar bears and other Arctic animals; during the summer, kids can watch a remote video of divers collecting samples from the bottom of the lake in front of the aquarium. (What's down there? Bottles, jars, rocks covered with mussels, and some hard-to-make-out marine life.)

Your family can also sign up for entertaining weekend workshops like Splendid Sharks, which examines how sharks can locate food miles away and reveals which kinds of sharks like plankton and which have a taste for . . . well, meat. Kids get a chance to meet live and preserved sharks and view the behaviors of sharks on display in the galleries. The Dinner at the North Pole workshop lets preschool through second-grade kids discover how Arctic animals find their food in a land of ice and snow.

In the summer the aquarium is one of the sponsors of the Summer World's Tour, a weeklong camp that lets kids study different aspects of the natural world at all three nearby museums: the aquarium, the planetarium, and the Field. Kids have fun exploring topics like Giants of the Universe, a fabulous week spent among whales, prehistoric swimming reptiles, dinosaurs, and on Jupiter. Registration for this program takes place at the aquarium.

To find out about aquarium programs, pick up a copy of *Aquascope* at the aquarium information booth, or request a copy from the Education Department.

Logistics

Because the oceanarium is so popular, it's best to purchase tickets in advance. You can reserve them through Ticketmaster at 902-1500. The extra service charge is annoying, but for families with children, it's better than standing in a long line.

The aquarium's Soundings restaurant and Bubble Net cafeteria both offer wonderful views of Monroe Harbor and downtown Chicago.

A handicapped/stroller entrance is located south of the Shedd Aquarium's main entrance. Wheelchairs are available, but please note that strollers are not permitted in the oceanarium. A stroller check is available.

The John G. Shedd Aquarium is open seven days a week from 9:00 A.M. to 6:00 P.M. It is closed on Christmas Day and New Year's Day. Admission to the aquarium and oceanarium is $8 for adults, $6 for children 3–11. Admission to the aquarium only is $4 for adults, $3 for children 3–11. On Thursday, when the aquarium is free, admission to the oceanarium is $4 for adults and $3 for children.

John G. Shedd Aquarium
1200 S. Lake Shore Drive
General information: 939-2438
Program and workshop information: 939-2426, ext. 3420

5

Culture for Kids

In a city bursting with great cultural institutions, there are a million ways to introduce kids to the arts. From classical music and opera to foot-stompin' bluegrass to the legacy of Frank Lloyd Wright and the vibrancy of outdoor art festivals, there are long-term classes and flashy special events for your whole family to enjoy!

Classical Music for Kids
Chicago Symphony Orchestra

Children under 8 are not allowed to attend regular performances of the Chicago Symphony Orchestra–and no wonder. Despite their beauty, performances that finish late in the evening will tax the manners and patience of even the best-behaved child.

Fortunately, the CSO's Family Series offers a wonderful way to introduce kids (and their parents) to classical music and the orchestra. Offered three Saturday mornings during the symphony season, each one-hour program mixes a variety of media to add a visual element to an otherwise aural experience. The result animates instruments, stories, and composers in a memorable, enjoyable way.

One program, focusing on Stravinsky's *Firebird Suite*, dramatizes the story with shadow puppets operated by the Underground Railway Theater. *Beethoven Lives Upstairs* tells

Beethoven's story, examines how he composed music, and features well-known Beethoven works.

Each program is offered twice, at 11:00 A.M. and at 12:30 P.M. Tickets range from $10 to $20 a performance. You can subscribe to the whole series, or buy tickets for one performance only.

There is no minimum age for these performances, but children who are between 4 and 12 will enjoy them most. If your child is over 8 and has an interest in classical music, try subscribing to the Sunday afternoon series of five, full-length concerts. Friday afternoon concerts are another good choice. According to the CSO, the Friday concerts are popular with members of high-school bands and orchestras, who often attend these performances as a group.

Chicago Symphony Orchestra
220 S. Michigan Avenue
435-8122

Grant Park Concert Society

The Grant Park Concert Society offers many ways for your family to experience classical music, absolutely free. On almost any summer evening, you can listen to beautiful music on a blanket under the stars, and the Concerts for Kids, Too! series is specially programmed to delight children.

During these concerts, the conductor speaks directly to youngsters about what they will hear. The conductor may focus your child's attention on a certain section of the orchestra, or a theme that is repeated throughout a piece. Some concerts feature very accessible music like the themes from *Beauty and the Beast* and *Jurassic Park*. Many showcase the talents of young Chicago residents who perform in the Chicago Youth Symphony Orchestra, the Merit Music Program's chamber and string ensembles, and the Chicago Children's Choir.

Most Concerts for Kids, Too! are held on midweek mornings, so that day-care and summer camp groups can attend. There are a handful of evening and Sunday afternoon performances. On days when there is no morning kids' performance scheduled, you can still enjoy classical music over lunch during the Grant Park Symphony's rehearsal, held between 10:00 A.M. and 1:00 P.M. Your kids can hear the conductor giving final notes about the pieces the orchestra will play that night or the next. Call before you pack your lunch to make sure a rehearsal is scheduled.

Grant Park Concert Society
520 S. Michigan Avenue #343
294-2420

Pick-Staiger Concert Hall
Kids Fare Program

Pick-Staiger Concert Hall at Northwestern University offers eight to ten special programs each year at a very family-friendly price. Tickets are just $2 for children under 12, and only $3 for adults. (If you are affiliated with Northwestern University in any way, they cost even less.)

These one-hour programs are held Saturday mornings at 10:30 A.M. in the concert hall. The concerts blend music, dance, and theater in an interactive performance led by a faculty artist who engages kids in making music and appreciating the results. Typical concerts have included African American instruments and music; featured the tuba, bassoon, and other orchestra giants; or offered kids a chance to direct a symphonic wind ensemble or dance along with a ballet corps. The annual Christmas family concert features selections from the *Nutcracker* and other familiar classical holiday pieces.

Each fall season kicks off with the annual Wildcats on Parade, when kids can march in formation with the Northwestern University marching band at an NU football game. Whether you attend one concert or the whole season, your family will absolutely love learning about music through this imaginative series.

Pick-Staiger Concert Hall
Northwestern University
1977 S. Campus Drive
Evanston
(708) 491-5441

●●●●●●●●●●●●●●●●●●●●●●●●●●●●●●●●●●

Strike Up the Band

Your tot can join the Northwestern University Wildcat Marching
Band for a day and savor the thrill of leading marching musicians
across Evanston's Dyche Stadium during a pregame performance.

Kids 3 to 10 can bring and play any instrument they please:
plastic drums, kazoos, bugles, tambourines, rhythm sticks, maracas,
pot lids, or any object that can make a loud, obnoxious noise.
(Kazoos are available for kids who leave their instruments at home.)

Before the grand march, children meet the band members. As
everyone sings "Who are the people in your marching band?" (based
on guess which *Sesame Street* song) the sections introduce
themselves and their instruments and play excerpts from their
half time show. When the formalities are over, kids, band members,
and drum majorettes gather at the goal post and march down the
field to the other goal post. The band members look sharp in their
uniforms, but otherwise it's a motley crew of toddlers, big kids,
and parents pushing strollers and making all the noise they can!

Tickets are available at the stadium on game day, so you can
wait and see what the weather is like before committing your
family to attending. If the weather is good and your kids like football,
buy a reduced-price ticket and stay for the game.

●●●●●●●●●●●●●●●●●●●●●●●●●●●●●●●●●●●●

A member of the Northwestern Wildcats marching band assists a young recruit during Wildcats on Parade. *Courtesy Northwestern University.*

Music and Movement

Old Town School of Folk Music

For lively, distinctly nonclassical concerts and kids programming, the Old Town School of Folk Music has no peer.

If they are willing to appear in public with their parents, preteens and teens can skip the kid's shows and go directly to OTS's regular concerts, where foot-stompin' performances by musicians from Finland, South America, and Madagascar will captivate the whole family. (If you do take younger children, choose a seat on the aisle so you can get to the bathroom easily.)

The OTS Children's Concert Series painlessly introduces children to a wide range of musical styles. These weekend afternoon concerts showcase talents like folksinger Tom Paxton, the zany duo Trout Fishing in America, or Latin American musicians. No one sits still at these concerts. There's plenty of give-and-take and parent-and-child play in each show. Tickets are $6 each.

Every Saturday morning, families with kids under 5 can enjoy an hour of song and dance during the Family Jamboree. Beginning at 10:00 A.M., the halls fill with the voices of kids and parents singing along to "The Barney Song" and other well-known tunes. Admission is $4 for adults, and $3 for kids over 12 months. No reservations are needed.

Among families, OTS is best known for its popular Wiggleworms classes, a parent-child music and motion class geared to very young children. In this gentle forty-five-minute class, toddlers and parents sing classics like "Wheels on the Bus," and kids get a chance to try out small percussion instruments. Even a 6-month-old baby can enjoy the Wiggleworms program, which offers separate groups for children 6–12 months, 1–2 years, and 2–3 years. Classes are offered at the OTS and at satellite locations in Pilsen, Evanston, and Hinsdale. Classes are available in Spanish in Pilsen and on Saturday at the school.

If you've never "wiggled," you can see what the excitement is all about during Wiggleworm Family Night—an evening of songs, finger play, and dances for the whole family offered every other month from 6:30 to 7:15 P.M. After a Family Night, you'll want to register your kids for the next session! Admission to Family Night is $3 for kids and $4 for adults.

The Old Town School of Folk Music offers many, many music classes for children. There are even guitar classes for kids and parents, so you can accompany your children to "Wheels on the Bus" and other favorite kid ditties!

It's hard to park in the neighborhood around OTS, but parking is available in a lot on the southwest corner of Kenmore and Clybourn Avenues, about four blocks away from the OTS. The parking problem may ease up in 1996, when OTS moves to new quarters in the former Hild Library at Lincoln and Wilson Avenues. But even when the school moves north, the Armitage Avenue building will remain the headquarters for Wiggleworms and other children's programs.

Old Town School of Folk Music
909 W. Armitage Avenue
525-7793

Jesse White Tumblers

It's not really music, it's not quite dance—but it's definitely worth seeing! The talented teens in the Jesse White Tumblers seem to shrug off gravity itself during their death-defying performances at Chicago summer festivals.

If your kids have never seen these red-clad athletes in action, make it a priority next summer. They'll thrill as these kids rely on small trampolines, highly conditioned muscles, and sheer nerve to execute incredible feats in midair. Watch as the tumblers take turns flipping over a human pyramid that grows higher and higher until it's hard to believe anyone will be able to leap— much less flip—so high and so far.

But somehow, the kids pull off every stunt every time, and without injury. Like the rest of the crowd, your kids will break into enthusiastic applause for the derring-do of the Jesse White Tumblers.

To find out where the Jesse White Tumblers are performing, check the weekend sections of the *Sun-Times* and *Tribune*, or call 266-7498.

Happiness Club

The Happiness Club is a joyous bunch of kids from all walks of life who endure a rigorous weekly practice schedule in order to stage high-voltage, upbeat shows for kids throughout Chicago.

Although its thirty-two members come from different neighborhoods and suburbs, and ethnic and economic backgrounds, they are united in their desire to write and perform songs and raps about values and ethics. Their lyrics cover everything from saving the environment, avoiding drugs, and staying in school to stopping street crime.

You can see them on the Bozo Show, at Comiskey Park, and at outdoor festivals like the Taste of Chicago, Oz Park Festival, and the International Children's Festival. They are regulars on the weekend Spanish-language TV show *Brechita 44*, and several of their members have roles on shows like the *Cosby Show* and *Ghostwriter*.

You can also drop by Revere Park (2509 W. Irving Park Road) any Sunday and watch them rehearse—especially if your child has a hankering to join the group. (Boys are especially needed.) Rehearsals start at 10:00 A.M. and run till 4:30 P.M. If your child wants to audition, call founder Gigi Faraci Harris first to set up an appointment, and make sure your child is prepared to perform a song, a dance, or a scene when the group's rehearsal is over.

The Happiness Club is always looking for new material, so if your young genius doesn't want to join the touring cast, he or she can submit poems, raps, and prose that can be turned into songs.

For more information about the Happiness Club, call Gigi Faraci Harris at (708) 843-3970.

Art on the Street

If it's July or August, your kids can see art in action at Gallery 37, a project of the City of Chicago Department of Cultural Affairs.

Every summer on block 37—bounded by Washington, State, Dearborn, and Randolph Streets—550 young people ages 14–21 serve as apprentice artists who are paid to create art in front of the public. For eight weeks they paint, draw, sculpt, write, dance, and perform for anyone who visits the Gallery 37 tents.

Your kids will be attracted by the creative energy that pours out of Gallery 37. It's fascinating to watch these young artists at work, and wonderful to witness performances on the Gallery's Mainstage, where local dance and arts groups perform weekly.

Of course, it's more fun to make your own art. And that's what kids can do at the Outreach Tent, in which there are imaginative new ways to involve the public in creating art. During the summer of 1994, the Outreach Tent created the Chicago Wish Line. Everyone who visited was asked to write a wish on a laminated sheet that was hung up on clothesline outside the tent. Eventually, thousands of wishes—private and public, for personal gain, world peace, and racial harmony—fluttered in the wind. Be prepared to be amazed by the ingenious project that awaits you at the Outreach Tent.

On Saturdays, you and your kids can enjoy free art classes taught by instructors from the School of the Art Institute. From 10:00 A.M. to 4:00 P.M., you can learn printmaking, watercolor painting, ceramics, figure drawing, cloth printing, and, with the Old Town School of Folk Music, instrument making. All necessary materials are supplied.

Gallery 37 art lessons could be a one-day excursion, or your child could take them every Saturday. The same instructors teach the courses every week, so your child can build a relationship with a special teacher. Even very young children can enjoy scribbling or finger painting while older children and adults work on their masterpieces.

The artworks created by these talented apprentice artists of Gallery 37 are available for sale inside Gallery 37 or at the Gallery 37 store in the Stouffer Riviera Hotel at One West Wacker Drive. The young artists are paid an hourly wage, so proceeds from their art go to fund the program.

If your teen is interested in joining the Gallery 37 crew, call early in the winter to find out how and where to get an application. (If your teen is a writer or musician, Gallery 37 also has a literary program, a journalism program, and a music program in which teens perform in a Latin salsa band throughout the city.) Applications must be accompanied by a recommendation from your teen's art teacher. All applicants take a basic English test and an arts aptitude test that focuses on basic skills like drawing figures or a still life.

Applications are reviewed by a board comprised of the teaching organizations that work with Gallery 37, including the School of the Art Institute, Lill Street Gallery, and the Sherwood Conservatory of Music. Teens will be admitted to the program by late spring, and start working as apprentice artists in July.

Gallery 37
State Street between Randolph and Washington Streets
For information about Outreach Tent activities,
call 744-8925
For information about applications, call 744-1430

After School Arts and Crafts

Chicago boasts many regional art centers, where your child can discover the world of art through imaginative and often very reasonably priced programs.

The **Beverly Arts Center** (2153 W. 111th Street, 445-3838) on the South Side offers instruction for children in ballet, jazz, tap dance, drawing and painting, cartooning, creative story writing, and drama, as well as guitar, piano, and violin.

At the **Hyde Park Art Center** (5307 S. Hyde Park Boulevard, 324-5520), kids can take after-school classes in painting, drawing, ceramics, photography, and cartooning. On Saturday and Sunday afternoons, the center sponsors family workshops where parents and children can work together to create origami figures, ceramics, paper, masks, and candles. During the summer, these two-hour workshops are often held outside in the park across the street (the one where the parrots live in the trees!). Outdoor workshops focus on making kites, boats, masks, and paper.

On the North Side, **Kids and Clay** (4905 N. Damen Avenue, 878-5821) offers classes in pottery, wheel throwing, and piano. A highlight here are the Christmas and Hanukkah ornament workshops, held twice during the holiday season. The ornaments have already been cut and fired into geese, menorahs, wreaths, trees, and other holiday figures, so parents and kids can spend the evening painting them with acrylics. (They make great gifts!) At Easter, families can work together to glaze beautiful ceramic eggs.

A specialty of the **Lill Street Gallery** (1021 W. Lill Street, 477-6185) is School's Out Camp. On Martin Luther King Day, President's Day, and Columbus Day, kids can create art from 9:00 A.M. to 3:00 P.M.—lots more fun than day care! Preregistration is necessary for these camps, as well as Winter Camp (held during the winter break) and Summer Camp. Lill Street offers after-school and weekend classes in clay, cartooning, painting, drawing, and multimedia for children 2 to 12 years old. Art birthday parties are also available.

The **Chicago Park District** offers many, many arts programs, including pottery, drawing and painting, arts and crafts, and music lessons! Call the District's Communication Office at 294-2490 to find the art classes close to you.

A Store, a Classroom, a Party Center

At City Crafts on Lincoln Avenue, kids can plunk down and make a wonderful craft project in just a few minutes—and take the finished project home!

Founded by Catherine Cox, former special projects coordinator for the *Reader*, this wonderful store offers an abundance of craft supplies: tissue paper, glitter, pipe cleaners, tempera paint, and kits for making Native American moccasins, totem poles, and hogans, as well as African masks, crystal radio sets, puppets, and hundreds more items.

With Catherine's Make It and Take It program, your child can paint beads, a pencil box, or a flowerpot; construct a wild animal mask; decorate a picture frame or a candle; marbleize paper;

paint with sand; or try copper tooling. No preregistration is required, but call first to make sure there's space, since this is turning into a popular birthday party spot. A Make It and Take It project costs $2.50 per child plus materials, or about $5 or $6 total.

This is an especially nice activity if your family schedule is too busy for a long-term crafts class commitment, or if your child wants to try out a couple crafts before settling down to one skill. If your child does want to take a crafts class, City Crafts offers plenty. There's an eight-week preschool craft program for kids under 5 and their parents or caregivers, and an after-school club for older children that offers a weekly project and juice-and-cookie snack. Even grown-ups can enjoy learning basic beading or mastering the secrets of trendy faux paint techniques.

If you don't have time for a project and only need to shop, seat your kids at the rubber stamp table and let them stamp away while you buy craft supplies.

So far this store is wildly successful with the families who patronize it—despite the dire predictions of craft industry professionals who told Cox that crafts stores simply couldn't succeed in the city. Stop by or call to get your name on the mailing list, and enjoy year-round arts and crafts adventures. City Crafts is closed Mondays.

City Crafts
2736 N. Lincoln Avenue
472-7911

A Kid's Take on Frank Lloyd Wright

Kids can learn to appreciate the legacy of Frank Lloyd Wright without suffering through a tour intended for grown-ups through the tours for kids *by* kids offered by the Frank Lloyd Wright Home and Studio.

The Home and Studio's specially trained junior tour leaders are middle schoolers who can help kids see things from Wright's point of view. They'll show your kids the patterns of shapes used

A Junior Interpreter points out features of the dining room in the Frank Lloyd Wright house in Oak Park. *Courtesy the Frank Lloyd Wright Home and Studio Foundation.*

in each room, and point out details like the tree growing in the passageway and the piano suspended over the stairs. They'll explain how Wright's palette and structures were influenced by his love of nature, music, and things Japanese.

Tour leaders will also grab your kids' attention by divulging how the Wright children turned their home's unique features into a romper room. (Which was harder: restoring the studio to its current state, or keeping the Wright kids from trashing it the first time around?) Kid audiences hear how the Wright kids had pillow fights over the wall separating the two bedrooms, and how the older boys who brought dates into the living room inglenook were received with a shower of spitballs from above.

Regular tours of the Frank Lloyd Wright Home and Studio are given Monday through Friday at 11:00 A.M., 1:00 P.M., and 3:00 P.M. On Saturday and Sunday from 11:00 A.M. to 4:00 P.M., tours are offered continuously. Admission to these tours is $6 for adults, $3 for seniors and youths 6–14.

Junior Interpreter tours held January through November on the fourth Saturday of the month at 10:00 A.M., cost $1.50 for kids 6–14. Midweek tours can be arranged by calling ahead to request a Junior Interpreter. During December, these guides lead special Victorian Christmas tours through the Home and Studio.

The Frank Lloyd Wright Home and Studio also offers junior and senior high-school students a unique way to spend the summer. Its summer architectural workshops pair students with an architect and teacher to design and build a Usonian home, a small, modestly priced type of housing Wright developed in the forties. For extra inspiration, students work in Wright's drafting room and visit local architectural firms. Call the Home and Studio for details.

Frank Lloyd Wright Home and Studio
931 Chicago Avenue
Oak Park
(708) 848-1978

6

Once Upon
a Time

Books, Theater, and Film

Even in today's video age, the phrase "Once upon a time" still turns heads. Here are bookstores, libraries, book fairs, and film festivals whose spellbinding stories will charm your kids–plus places where your kids can tell a tale or two of their own!

Bookstore Story Hours

African American Images

African American Images bookstore offers a special story hour for children in kindergarten through fifth grade. On the first Saturday of the month at 2:00 P.M., children and guest readers gather to share contemporary and ancient African fables and myths.

African American Images
1909 W. Ninety-fifth Street
445-0322

Barnes & Noble

Barnes & Noble offers story hours Thursday at 4:00 P.M. and Saturday at 11:00 A.M. Your kids may be treated to an old classic like *The Red Balloon* or a new title like *Molly's Pilgrim*. Call before you go, just to make sure story hour hasn't been bumped by a special event or rescheduled during a busy holiday sales season.

Barnes & Noble Booksellers
659 Diversey Parkway
871-9004

The Children's Bookstore

Besides offering an astonishing collection of books and toys, cassettes, multicultural materials, books on parenting and child care, and a basement entirely devoted to books for 8- to 15-year-olds, The Children's Bookstore offers story hour for young children every Tuesday, Wednesday, and Thursday at 10:30 A.M.

There's always something happening here. For older kids, weekend and after-school events feature characters like Curious George, musicians like Ella Jenkins and the Chicago Children's Choir, and authors like Brian Jacques, whose Redwall adventure series is all the rage among grade-school kids. And celebrations abound. The Children's Bookstore blends stories, music, and ritual to celebrate everything from Christmas and Kwanzaa and Passover to April Fool's Day.

To stay on top of all these events, ask the store to send you its monthly *Children's Bookstore Bulletin*.

Children's Bookstore
2465 N. Lincoln Avenue
248-BOOK

57th Street Books

Every Wednesday morning at 10:30 A.M., a 57th Street staff member reads a mix of old and new books to toddlers and young preschoolers. On Saturday mornings, the staff selects books that appeal to a slightly older audience of preschoolers and kindergartners. Story time lasts an hour, or until children are too restless to continue; then everyone enjoys a free cup of hot chocolate–the libation of choice even when it's sweltering outside!

57th Street Books
1301 E. Fifty-seventh Street
684-1300

The Magic Tree Bookstore

Oak Park's premier children's bookstore offers story hour every Tuesday from 10:00 to 10:30 A.M. Each week's stories revolve around a theme, like owl stories, Hanukkah stories, or Eric Carle stories. Books related to the week's theme are discounted 10 percent.

The Magic Tree Bookstore frequently invites authors and illustrators to readings and book signings. Other special events include bookmark design contests, birthday parties for storybook celebrities like the Very Hungry Caterpillar, and a unique Family Poetry Slam. Modeled after the hip slams held in adults-only venues like the Green Mill and the World Tattoo Parlor, this poetry slam invites kids, moms, dads, uncles, and aunts to read their own works or their favorite poems.

The Magic Tree Bookstore
141 N. Oak Park Avenue
Oak Park
(708) 848-0770

Women & Children First

Professional storyteller and co-owner Linda Bubon leads Kiddie Lit for City Kids every Wednesday morning from 10:00 to 10:30 A.M. With lively stories, finger plays, and silly poems, her presentations are a wonderful interactive story time for very young children. Her story hours offer a mix of new stories and classic tales, many of which feature strong and lively girls.

In fact, strong and lively girls is a big theme at Women & Children First. If you're at a loss when it comes to good stories with great girl heroines, check out the store's Great Girl Stories section for inspiring alternatives to the latest volume in the Babysitter's Little Sisters Club. Women & Children First also has books on issues like adoption, disabilities, divorce, gay/lesbian parenting, classic parenting problems like potty training and new sibling arrival, in addition to pop up books, activity books, multicultural folktales, and a collection of the best children's literature for babies to teens.

Women & Children First
5233 N. Clark Street
769-9299

The 57th Street Children's Book Fair

To introduce your child to Clifford the Big Red Dog, or let her visit the cozy room depicted in *Goodnight, Moon*, don't miss the Lollapalooza of children's literature: the 57th Street Children's Book Fair.

Held every September since 1985, the fair brings to life the stars of children's literature: Paddington Bear, Cinderella, Bunnicula, Clifford, Ms. Frizzle, Pippi Longstocking, and other favorites, who lead off the 1:00 P.M. parade down Fifty-seventh Street and then linger to work the crowd. These life-size heroes make an especially big impression on children under 6, but even older kids will enjoy meeting characters they have known and loved.

Especially enchanting are the kid-sized storybook rooms where tots can wander through scenes from their favorite books. The dioramas show rooms featured in *Peter Pan*, *Where's Spot?*, *Where the Wild Things Are*, and *Goodnight, Moon*.

Throughout the afternoon, families can enjoy free performances by storytellers, musicians, and dancers, or stop to make a hat, have their faces painted, or write their names in hieroglyphics at one of the craft tables.

Everything is free except the books, and many of these are very inexpensive. The fair, cosponsored by the Mayor's Office of Special Events, is a showcase for Chicago booksellers who specialize in children's literature. You'll find stacks of new and used paperbacks, hardcovers, and audiocassette tapes for children of all ages, from general bookstores as well as those that focus on books by and for African Americans or Latinos.

To help you find the best books for your kids, the fair is staffed by librarians, publishers, academics, and other children's literature specialists who can help you find books on subjects ranging from potty training to death, divorce, and step families. The specialists wear name tags that identify their area of expertise, and if you're looking for a particular expert, the fair's helpful staff can lend a hand.

The 57th Street Children's Book Fair is held on a late September Sunday. For more information, call 702-6421.

A World of Tales at the Chicago Public Library

With eighty branches throughout the city and a deluxe downtown venue, the Chicago Public Library is a great place for kids to meet the giants, imps, and heroines of children's literature.

On the mezzanine of the Harold Washington Library Center, the Thomas Hughes Children's Library offers many cozy, colorful nooks where kids can curl up and read or listen. You can come for a special event, or stop by anytime to check out books from its fabulous children's literature collection. Wednesday and Friday mornings at 10:15 A.M., a story time extravaganza of puppets and stories takes over the bright yellow "story stairs," a cheerful, kid-scale performance area. The Wednesday stories are for 3- to 5-year-old kids; Friday morning stories are for 6- to 8-year-olds. The same stories are presented throughout the month.

On Saturday afternoon, a variety of programs are presented in the library's Program Room. Your kids may watch a popular puppet play, hear a story, or watch a family video from the library's Film/Video Department. Programs revolve around seasons, ethnic and holiday celebrations, or favorite kid topics like dinosaurs. Events funded through the library's Nature Connections Program usually feature a nature-related craft or a naturalist-led workshop on plants or animals.

These programs are free and open to all young children; no reservations are required. If you're a big fan of library programs, ask to have your name added to the mailing list, so you can receive a monthly bulletin of children's activities.

Your local library is another good source of free children's programs. Even the smallest branches offer preschool story time, and many bring in special performances and craft activities. Regional libraries like Conrad Sulzer on North Lincoln Avenue have excellent collections of children's books, videos, and audiocassettes, and offer free after-school and summer movies for kids.

Thomas Hughes Children's Library
Harold Washington Library Center
400 S. State Street
747-4200

Onstage and Backstage

Dozens of local theaters offer wonderful children's programming. Your best source of information on plays and musicals for children is *Chicago Parent*, which publicizes performances for children by groups like the Chicago Children's Theatre, the Lincolnshire Marriott, PIE Story Theatre, and the Player's Workshop Children's Theater. You can find this monthly guide wherever parents gather (day-care centers, schools, children's resale shops, etc.).

Many of these performances include a question-and-answer session in which kids can meet the actors, talk about their feelings, learn a few secrets of stagecraft, or even take a peek backstage.

But some kids aren't satisfied with seeing a play: they want to put on their *own* show. Here's where your stagestruck child can find training in acting and stagecraft:

The **Old Town School of Folk Music** teaches musical theater skills to kids from 5 to 8 years of age, who make their own costumes and perform a musical commissioned especially for the OTS. (Performances of the musicals, *The Blue Dog* and *Doggone Frog*, are also open to children.) Call 525-7793 for details on after-school classes and Musical Theatre Summer Camp.

The **Sherwood Conservatory**'s Stageworks introduces music, theater, and movement to kids ages 5 to 12. Kids learn acting, singing, set and costume design, and mount a fully staged performance. Sherwood Scene Shop teaches 10- to 12-year-olds the basics of acting through movement, discussion, theater games, and improvisation. Kids create and present their own play at the end of the term. Call the Sherwood Conservatory (1014 S. Michigan Avenue) at 427-6267.

In its classes for kids ages 9 through 18, the **Piven Theatre** Workshop in Evanston teaches a blend of improvisation and story theater techniques that encourage a youths' imagination and sense of play. Although the Piven Young People's Company does give performances, the program emphasizes process over performance and group collaboration over individual talents. Call (708) 866-6597.

Teens can take a special Musical Theatre Workshop through the Community Music Division of the **DePaul University School of Music**. Call the Community Music Division, 362-5343.

Acting classes for teens are offered by the **Goodman Theatre** staff at Brainerd Park (1246 W. Ninety-second Street, 233-6090) and Kelvyn Park (4438 W. Wrightwood Avenue, 252-8547), and by the **Raven Theatre** at Pottawattomie Park (7340 N. Rogers Avenue, 743-4313).

The **Organic Theater**'s Young Actors Program offers acting classes for kids ages 3 to 18, including children with physical and mental disabilities. Young children learn in a nurturing environment that culminates in a performance before friends and family. Older kids dreaming of careers in theater can take more demanding classes that teach professional skills. Call 883-0846.

By the way, even if your child doesn't end up taking an acting class, your family can enjoy these troupes' performances for little or no charge!

Why Kids Should Go to the Organic Theater

Children should go to the Organic Theater because it is a lot of fun. It is a lot of fun because you do a lot of things there, like play theater games, make friends, do a play on a certain theme, and have a great teacher. You get to play and rehearse in front of theater lights on a stage in costumes. You might feel nervous when you are acting in front of a bunch of people, but once you get the hang of it, it becomes natural.

The littler kids get to play more and easier theater games. You will either do a short play or you won't do a play at all. The older kids will do much harder theater games and a longer play. I think you should go to the Organic Theater because you will have a lot of fun and if you are bored it will save you.

—Jason Gannett
Uptown

Kid Film

Looking for great movies for kids?

The **Omnimax Theater** at the Museum of Science and Industry (684-1414) offers consistently high-quality films on topics that appeal to adults and children. To see an Omnimax movie during the day you need to purchase a combination movie-theater ticket at the main entrance to the Museum of Science and Industry. Some evening shows are also available. For ticket availability, call 684-1414, extension 2521. To reserve tickets in advance, call 684-1414, extension 2290 or Ticketmaster at 902-1500.

During the Chicago Cultural Center's **City Child in Summer Film Festival**, your family can see great films like *Doctor Dolittle* and *National Velvet* absolutely free. Films are shown at the Cultural Center (78 E. Washington Street) on summer Saturdays at 2:00 P.M. Call 744-1424 for a schedule.

The **Chicago Public Library** also shows free films at its many branches. Regional libraries like Conrad Sulzer show after-school children's movies practically every week. The Thomas Hughes Children's Library in the Harold Washington Library Center shows selections from the library's Film/Video Department during its monthly Family Video Program, suggested for families with children over 6. Call 747-4200 for information.

For home viewing, join **Facets Multimedia** (1517 W. Fullerton Avenue, 281-9075). Their collection of children's videos is the largest around. Busy parents can even rent videos by mail—especially convenient if you don't live in the Facets neighborhood.

Each October, Facets sponsors the **Chicago International Children's Film Festival**, a ten-day festival of movies for children by directors from around the world. For less than the cost of a standard first-run movie, your kids can sample fine animated shorts and full-length features written, acted, and produced specifically for children. Most of the films and videos are best suited for children from 6 to 12 years of age; a handful are appropriate for very young children or teens.

The festival's animated and live-action films and videos are carefully selected by several panels of judges, including one made up of fifty children. If your kid knows the kind of movies he likes, and why, there may be a place for him on the festival's junior panel of judges.

Your child can audition for the panel in June, when a large crowd of children gathers to view and judge a film. Based on their responses, Facets Multimedia selects children who express themselves well and can explain why a film does or does not appeal to them.

The fifty kids who are selected spend six days in August watching the final candidates for the festival. (Two adult juries composed of filmmakers, educators, and parents make the first cut.) A panel of 10- to 13-year-olds watch full-length features or a compilation of shorts; the 6- to 9-year-olds watch shorts.

After the kids view the films, the jury director asks them questions that get their wheels turning, and they write their responses on an evaluation form.

Many of the children on the jury return year after year. In one family of film buffs, every kid is a jury member! To find out when the next auditions are scheduled, call Facets at 281-9075.

7

Maritime Chicago

Chicago offers plenty of beachfront and lakeside family fun. From sandy beaches and shallow inlets to pint-size opportunities for sailing, rowing, canoeing, and fishing, maritime Chicago is a paradise just waiting to be explored!

Family Beaches

Scattered along Chicago's twenty-nine-mile shoreline are thirty-one beaches where you and your kids can swim, play, toss Frisbees, or just loll in the sun. Like people, each beach has its own personality and its own devotees. Here are some of the best for families with children.

Pebble Beach. Also known as the Forty-ninth Street Beach, this one comes recommended by Hyde Park parents who know it as a safe, quiet haven for kids under 5. Its pebble-covered shore fascinates little kids, who can spend hours examining the pebbles and polished glass to find favorites to take home. A lifeguard is present, but there are no amenities except an outdoor washroom you should use at your own discretion. Reach Pebble Beach by crossing Lake Shore Drive on the Fifty-first Street pedestrian bridge, and walking north.

The Point. Hyde Park's favorite picnic spot, the Point offers a great view of downtown but has no beach area. Older children with strong swimming skills can swim off the rocks when lifeguards are present. The closest bathrooms are in a nearby field house.

Twelfth Street Beach. This cozy family favorite can be a destination all its own or a nice treat after a day at the museums. It lies in a horseshoe that runs from the Adler Planetarium to the mouth of Burnham Harbor—almost directly underneath the flight path for Meigs Field! Until the airport closes in 1997, your kids can enjoy splashing in the water as private jets roar overhead. When swimming gets dull, you can walk along the water's edge around the planetarium, take a Shoreline Sightseeing Cruise, or dry off, clean up, and go see the sky show.

Twelfth Street Beach has changing facilities, bathrooms, vending machines, and is attended by a lifeguard. To get there, drive or walk east from Lake Shore Drive on Solidarity Drive. Meter parking is sometimes available, but it's easier to pay $4 and park in a lot. Park your car directly in line with the Meigs Field landing strip, and planes will land practically on top of you—an exciting illusion for the young set.

Montrose Beach. This big, wide beach offers plenty of picnic areas, parking, and full bathroom and changing facilities—plus the excitement of watching windsurfers maneuvering off its shore. Because it's also popular with jet skiers, it can get noisy. (Jet skiers pose no threat to young swimmers, though, because law forbids them to come within fifty yards of swimmers.)

Rogers Park Street-end Beaches. Between Thorndale Avenue in Edgewater and Howard Street in Rogers Park run a dozen tiny, street-end beaches that make perfect destinations for families. Leone Beach, Hartigan Beach, Howard Beach, and others like them are so small they seem like private beaches. These quiet little spots, so remote from the hustle and bustle of the city, have only two drawbacks: parking can be hard, and there are no bathrooms. Go before you get there, and look for parking west of Sheridan Road.

Loyola Park Beach. This big, friendly beach boasts a wonderful playground and a lovely tree-shaded promenade where kids can walk, bike, or skate. There are bathrooms in the nearby Loyola Park field house, and great food in the Heartland at the Beach snack stand. When the beach gets boring, your family can walk south a bit and watch the Rainbow Fleet sailboats and catamarans sailing off North Shore Beach.

Beach Blanket Babylon: The Chicago Park District Junior Lifeguard Program

Young beach bums who love swimming, sunning, and sailing can spend the summer at the beach simply by enrolling in the Park District Aquatics Camp.

Actually, Aquatics Camp sets kids up for several years on the beach, because this unique summer program grooms 8- to 16-year-olds for careers as Park District lifeguards. Kids meet daily from 10:00 A.M. to 4:00 P.M. to work on their swimming skills, learn how to use all types of lifeguard equipment and techniques, and master the basics of sailing. At Leone Beach in Rogers Park, kids can even water-ski!

Aquatics Camps and the Junior Lifeguard Program are offered at Leone Beach, Hartigan Beach, Montrose Beach, North Avenue Beach, Twelfth Street Beach, Fifty-seventh Street Beach, South Shore Beach, and Calumet Beach. According to Park District staff, Leone, Hartigan, and Calumet fill quickly, but there are generally plenty of openings at the other beaches.

For information about Aquatics Camps and the Junior Lifeguard Program, call the Park District's Beaches & Pools Division at 747-0832. Their personnel can also tell you about the indoor lifeguard program, offered year-round at all twenty-three of the district's indoor pools.

Lakefront Strolls

"Passive recreation" is a fancy name for just hanging out and enjoying the scene. Chicago's lakefront is one enormous passive recreation plaza—perfect for family strolls by day or by night.

A walk by any harbor will delight kids who revel in things nautical. There's the crisp white and blue of sails and canvas, and the constant clink of fittings against mast. There are multimillion-dollar yachts to admire, tiny dinghies to watch, and aggressive seagulls to feed. At Belmont Harbor, kids can watch as dry-docked boats are wheeled over to the crane that gently lifts and lowers them into the water.

One of the nicest strolls is along Monroe Harbor. Linger on any summer Friday afternoon, and you can share in the excitement as sailors prepare for weekend voyages. Set your kids down by the tender office on Lake Shore Drive north of Monroe, and watch as gear and groceries are unloaded from cars and loaded onto the little tenders that carry sailors out to their boats' moorings. Each tender is numbered, so kids can keep track of which tender is where and how many trips each one makes. At the guest mooring area north of the tender office, you can watch owners fiddle with fittings and pile baggage onto boats tied up at the sidewalk. It's fun to speculate about the travelers and where they might be going. It's also fun to match the dry-docked dinghies lining the harbor with their big sister yachts in the harbor (each dinghy has the same name as its sister ship).

If you want to make an evening out of your harbor visit, catch the Shoreline cruise boat that leaves opposite Buckingham Fountain. This thirty-minute cruise will take you out among the sailboats and let your kids admire a late-afternoon view of the city. Stay until dark, and wrap up your harbor expedition by admiring Buckingham Fountain's wonderful water-and-light show, which runs May 1 through October 1 from 9:00 to 11:00 P.M.

Unless you want to depend on strolling food vendors and ice-cream trucks, you might want to bring along something to eat while harbor watching. There is no café or restaurant along this stretch of the lake, although there is a vending machine (and a portable toilet unit) next to the harbor office. Bathrooms are available across Lake Shore Drive in Daley Bicentennial Plaza (337 E. Randolph Street), open 7:00 A.M. to 10:00 P.M.

Sailing, Sailing,
Over the Bounding Main

Sailing often seems like the province of the wealthy and the leisured. Thanks to two community sailing programs, any family can enjoy sailing.

The Chicago Park District Rainbow Fleet

Your whole family can learn to sail, courtesy of the Rainbow Fleet, the Chicago Park District's community sailing program.

Sailing Lessons

The Rainbow Fleet offers group or individual lessons to any Chicago resident who is over 10 years old. A one-week session of dryland and on-the-water instruction costs a mere $85, and certifies you to rent one of the fleet's sixteen-foot catamarans or fourteen-foot single-hulled Bartletts.

A one-week group session includes five three-hour lessons conducted in a Bartlett 14. (Private lessons meet for an hour each day.) After an onshore introduction to the parts of a boat and the basics of sailing, you spend the week on the water. If you've mastered the basics by the end of the week, you'll be certified as a skipper, and you can take your family sailing anytime!

Lessons are offered at three locations: North Shore Beach (Pratt Avenue and Lake Michigan), South Shore Beach (Seventy-first Street and South Shore Drive), and Burnham Harbor (1362 S. Linn White Drive, south of the Adler Planetarium). Mom and Dad can take individual lessons at North Shore and South Shore Beaches, or group lessons at Burnham Harbor. Kids 10 to 16 can take the helm during afternoon Junior Lessons at North Shore and South Shore Beaches.

Lessons are offered weekly from the second week of June through the second week of August. To sign up, request a registration form from the Park District's Marine Department, and mail or bring it to the department. Because this program, like many Park District programs, is sadly underpublicized, there is plenty of room for new sailors, especially young ones. (There are plenty of scholarships, too.) Private lessons may be reserved as little as a week in advance.

Renting a Boat

You can take your kids out for a sail by renting a tiny Rainbow Fleet boat—a snug fourteen-footer with room for three—at North Shore or South Shore Beaches. Before you set sail, you'll be asked to show a certification card from the Park District, the American Youth Hostels, or another sailing organization. If you don't have a card, you'll be asked a few basic questions to determine your knowledge of sailing. Expect to be quizzed at length if you request the Hobie catamaran, or try to sail when the weather is rough. If the Fleet staff isn't convinced that you can sail, an instructor can sail with you for an additional $5.

While you're sailing, the Fleet staff will keep an eye on you to make sure everything is OK. You can only keep the boat for two hours, tops, so you probably won't get more than a mile offshore anyway.

On weekdays Rainbow Fleet boats can be rented for one or two hours at a time from 12:30 to 5:30 P.M. On weekends sailing starts at 11:15 A.M. and ends at 4:15 P.M. One hour in a Barnett costs $15, two hours costs $25. The catamaran costs $25 for an hour and $40 for two. Fees must be paid in cash and a $20 cash deposit is required. To make sure a boat will be available when your family arrives, call the beach and reserve one forty-eight hours ahead of your visit.

The Judd Goldman Adaptive Sailing Program

Through this program, funded by the Judd Goldman Adaptive Sailing Foundation and administered by the Chicago Park District, disabled youth and their families can enjoy the excitement of sailing. Its fleet of specially designed sailboats make it easy to transfer from wheelchair to counterweighted seats that allow sailors to maneuver the boat's lines, tillers, and riggings. Chest belts, waist belts, and life jackets prevent injuries, and each boat has an outboard motor and a marine radio that can be used to call for help in an emergency.

Adaptive sailing lessons are open to people with all sorts of disabilities, including paraplegia, quadriplegia, multiple sclerosis, muscular dystrophy, cerebral palsy, amputations, spina bifida, as well as learning, emotional, and developmental disabilities. The only requirement for participation is the ability to float calmly in the water for five minutes while wearing a life jacket.

Parents and family members may participate in the classes with their child. Qualified skippers with disabilities may rent the Freedom Independence 20s when they are not being used for instruction. (Skipper certification is earned after twenty-four hours of instruction, or two lesson cycles.) A weekly race series lets sailors with a competitive streak accumulate points to qualify for the Annual Goldman Cup Regatta and the North American Challenge Cup.

For more information about the Adaptive Sailing Program or Rainbow Fleet lessons and rentals, contact:

Chicago Park District
Sailing Program Coordinator
425 E. McFetridge Drive
747-0737

Sail Chicago

Another way to get your family on the water is for Mom or Dad to learn the ropes through American Youth Hostels. The AYH Sail Chicago program teaches the ins and outs of handling a Rhodes 19 to individuals over 16. These evening classes cost $300 and consist of four classroom lessons and ten two-hour lessons on the water. Once you're certified, you can check out boats from the AYH's collection of nineteen-, twenty-two-, and twenty-seven-foot boats—or bring your family along on a scheduled cruise of its thirty-foot boat.

Sail Chicago runs classes from Monroe, Belmont, and Montrose Harbors. Unlike the Park District sailing program, these classes fill up quickly (only 150 new sailors a year are certified). Register in January to ensure a spot for the following summer.

AYH also has an extensive canoeing program, and twice a year it offers canoeing lessons. Open to anyone over 10, the $50 course consists of an evening lecture, a Sunday paddling lesson, and a trip down the north branch of the Chicago River, starting at Skokie Lagoons. Once your family has mastered the basics, it's welcome to join regular AYH canoe trips on gentle, family-friendly waterways.

Don't forget that joining American Youth Hostels also qualifies your family to take advantage of the international network of safe, friendly, and inexpensive youth hostels. All told, there are 200 hostels in the United States and about 6,000 in seventy different countries, all ready to welcome your family on your out-of-Chicago adventures.

Sail Chicago
American Youth Hostels
3036 N. Ashland Avenue
327-8114

Canoeing and Kayaking

Think of canoeing, and you probably think of a trip to the Boundary Waters, or an expensive vacation to a western state. But your family can enjoy canoeing and kayaking without leaving Chicago at all, thanks to the Lincoln Park Boat Club.

Founded in 1908, the Boat Club runs the Boathouse on the Lincoln Park Lagoon, which runs nearly a kilometer along the west side of Lake Shore Drive starting at Fullerton Avenue. An annual family membership of $140 entitles you to a key to the Boathouse and full access to its collection of shells, canoes, and kayaks.

Families prepare for a day on the water at the Lincoln Park Boat Club.
Photo by Debbie Kotzen.

The shells are one-, two-, four-, and eight-person boats designed for the kind of Ivy League-style rowing indigenous to the East Coast. Unless you're grooming your kids to be champions on a college crew, you'll probably be more interested in using the canoes and kayaks. Children as young as 6 are welcome to join their families in these vessels, or they can take group or individual lessons (not included in the cost of membership) and master the Frenzies—stable, practically unsinkable kayaks designed especially for kids. Kids who want to race can graduate to special kid-proportioned racing kayaks called Minjas.

The sheltered water of the lagoon is a perfect place for kids to master boating. In fact, it was built for Chicago's rowing clubs after Lake Shore Drive cut off their access to the beach. Its no-wave, no-wake surface is always calm, placid, and very, very safe. And the Boat Club takes the extra safety step of insisting that all members use its log to sign themselves on and off the water.

Adults and children can also learn how to use sea kayaks, a skill that will come in handy if you ever want to go whale watching in the Puget Sound. Very accomplished adult and teen paddlers—

but not children—can take the sea kayaks out onto the lake via Diversey Harbor. When your family takes the plunge and buys its own kayak, you can store it in the Boathouse instead of your garage.

If your kids are intrigued by the idea of learning to paddle, stop by the Boathouse and give it a try. After you sign a release, you'll be ushered to an appropriate vessel, and pushed off. While there's no cost involved, a Boat Club member will need to be on hand to supervise you.

Finding the Boat Club is a challenge. You can see it quite clearly from the Drive, but its architects designed it to blend into the surrounding landscape. Drive south from Fullerton Avenue on Cannon Drive, and it will be on your left just after you pass the entrance to the Lincoln Park Zoo parking lot. It's the bunker-style building with trees and bushes growing up its sides.

The club's 300 members use the Boathouse from mid-March until November, when the dock comes off the water. If you stop by for a free paddle, go on a weekend or weekday evening when members are on hand. For information on joining, call the number below.

Even if you don't join the Boat Club, your family can enjoy the excitement of its annual Chicago Sprints Regatta, held the third Saturday in July. For one day you can feel what it's like to sit along Boston's Charles River and watch college crews from all over the Northeast—except in this case, the competitors come from rowing clubs all over the Midwest. Races start at 8:00 A.M. and last all day. Pick up a program and stand at the reviewing tent next to the Boathouse, in order to find out the specifics of each match.

Lincoln Park Boat Club
South of Fullerton Avenue on the Lincoln Park Lagoon
549-BOAT

Canoe and Kayak Central

There are twenty-four canoe and kayak clubs in Illinois, many of them in the Chicago area. These clubs offer formal teaching sessions in the spring, and schedule a variety of family outings to popular canoe routes like Skokie Lagoons on the Chicago River's north branch, the Des Plaines River, Salt Creek, Tampier Lake, and Busse Reservoir. The fastest way to find a club near you is to call Chicagoland Canoe Base, a one-of-a-kind store whose knowledgeable people can answer all your questions about canoeing and kayaking. The store also builds, rents, or sells just about everything you need to outfit your family for water sports. The store is open Monday through Saturday from 9:00 A.M. to 5:00 P.M., and Thursday until 9:00 P.M.

Chicagoland Canoe Base
4019 N. Narragansett Avenue
777-1489

Small Lakes and Little Boats

Think Lake Michigan is too big and too deep for your family? Then sail the calmer waters of the lakes in the Forest Preserve District of Cook County.

Canoes and rowboats can be rented at Busse Reservoir in the Ned Brown Preserve. This 590-acre lake, the largest in the Forest Preserve District, is quiet and shallow, with a maximum depth of fourteen feet and many marshy areas where the water is less than two feet deep.

Boats can be rented daily from April through September. (Weather permitting, weekend rentals are available during October.) Fishing enthusiasts take out boats as early as 6:00 A.M., but once the fishing crowd goes home there are plenty of boats available for families. On weekday afternoons you'll have no problem getting a boat; on weekends you can beat the crowd by calling ahead and reserving one.

Two-person canoes rent for $5 an hour or $15 a day. A small motorboat that comfortably fits three (four if you squeeze) rents for $8 an hour or $40 a day. Every boat comes with life jackets for everyone aboard. All boats must be in by 7:00 P.M.

Busse Reservoir is located on Higgins Road between I-90 and Arlington Heights. The entrance to the Boating Center is on

Higgins just east of I-90. Turn south onto the Forest Preserve Road and follow the boat rental signs. There are bathrooms and a concession stand where you can pick up snacks or microwave a sandwich.

Rowboats may also be rented at Maple and Tampier Lakes in the Palos Forest Preserve.

Busse Reservoir Boat Rental
Open Kitchens
Summer number: (708) 439-5008
Winter number: 666-5334

Maple and Tampier Lakes Boat Rental
T & M Lakes, Inc.
Summer number: (708) 361-1336

Smelt Fishing

Like the colorful rituals of baseball's Opening Day, lakefront bonfires and lanterns signal another great rite of spring in Chicago: smelt fishing.

Every April, when Chicago is still cold and gray, these little critters swim to shore to spawn. For a G-rated after-dark adventure, join the hundreds of fishing enthusiasts waiting to greet them with open nets and hearty appetites. You'll find that a night of smelt fishing yields quality time with the kids and a delicious meal to boot.

Smelt fishing is about the easiest kind of fishing there is. The only equipment you really need is a 5/8-inch or 3/4-inch gill net and two five-gallon plastic buckets—one for your gear and one for the fish you catch. (Smelt fishers who are over 16 also need a license, available for $13.00 at any bait shop.) All you have to do is take your net and buckets and scope out a spot around sunset. Some people like to set out their nets in sheltered places like Diversey and Montrose Harbors; others prefer the rock ledges that run from the Adler Planetarium to Thirty-first Street. The stunning view north from Burnham Harbor attracts more aesthetic-minded smelting families.

To fish, you drop your net and wait. If you're lucky, smelt will swim into your net and be trapped. If they don't, keep trying, or ask your neighbors for tips. After all, you'll be surrounded by experts who will be happy to share their secrets. Camaraderie runs with the smelt!

While your family waits, enjoy your surroundings. Everywhere there are blazing bonfires and cheerful families preparing to feast. Fixing smelt is easy; since you can eat their bones, all you have to do is trim off their heads and gut them, and you're ready to sauté, fry, steam, batter, or grill your fresh smelt for a delicious lakeside, nighttime picnic. You can also take them home to cook or freeze for a later banquet.

Yes, some smelt fishers would rather party than fish, but you can catch plenty of smelt and still be home by 9:00 P.M., before the boisterous types get out of hand. (They stay until 1:30 A.M., when it's smelt curfew time.)

Here are some hints to make your smelt-fishing night fun for everyone:

- Visit a bait shop to get a license, the right equipment, and a quick lesson in fishing for and cooking smelt.

- Dress warmly. It's still cold in April!

- Fish on a Thursday or Friday night to avoid the wilder weekend crowd.

- Get kids involved in tasks like setting out and emptying the nets, or holding the lantern.

- Keep a close eye on kids. The deep, cold, dark water is awfully dangerous if a child falls in. Fit everyone with life preservers and stay vigilant to prevent accidents.

- Enjoy!

8

Planes and Trains

Kids love engines on the grand scale: big trains, big planes, big bulldozers, monster trucks, stretch limousines. Any kind of enormous machinery also radiates enormous kid appeal. Likewise, small-scale equipment has its fans. Here are some places where kids can see big and little trains and planes, both at rest and (far better) in action.

Big Trains

Is your child mad for Thomas the Train Engine, or a devout model railroader? Try a Saturday trip to the Skybox for Rail Fans, on Eighteenth Street just east of Canal Street.

Owned and operated by the Twentieth Century Rail Club the Skybox is on the ninth floor of a building that sits due south of Union Station. It commands a spectacular view of Chicago's passenger rail tracks, plus a splendid view of the Loop from the south. From this vantage point, you can see all of Amtrak's Chicago operations (except northbound trains) plus commuter, freight, and rapid transit trains.

Settle yourselves in comfortable old chairs at the floor-to-ceiling windows, and let your child watch the trains come and go. On Saturday, you won't see many commuter trains, but you will see several dozen Amtrak trains arriving and departing, and plenty of solo engines running errands in the rail yard.

The commanding view of Union Station as seen from the Twentieth Century Railroad Club's Skybox for Railfans. *Photo by Stan Brandt.*

Your kids can see the building where engines are repaired, and watch for trains emerging from the small, narrow shed where they are washed. When a train approaches from the south, they'll see it turn and back into Union Station so that the engine is outside the station.

A short-wave radio tuned to the rail yard's frequency let's kids eavesdrop on engineers and brakemen shouting instructions to one another. If it's May or October, kids can also watch Chicago River bridges go up as sailboats move from dry docks to the lake in May, and back to the dry docks in October.

The Skybox is open Saturdays from noon to 5:00 P.M., from May 1 through October 31. Parking is located inside the building, and the elevator is attended. Entrance is free to members of the Twentieth Century Rail Club, and $3 for everyone else. Your host will be a genial board member of the 20th Century Rail Club, who can point out highlights to you and your kids. Coffee, soda, and cookies are available.

If your children *really* love trains, consider joining one of the Rail Club's day trips to the Milwaukee Circus Parade, Milwaukee

Summer Fest, or the East Troy Electric Railroad Museum in East Troy, Wisconsin. Schedules are available in the Skybox.

Twentieth Century Rail Club
329 W. Eighteenth Street
829-4500

Little Trains

The best train layout in town is the 3,000-square-foot model Santa Fe railway located in the Museum of Science and Industry's Railway Gallery.

Several trains run simultaneously on this intricate layout, which is controlled by a computer in the observation tower. Kids can watch signals flash off and on and see trains shunted to side tracks while another passes by. Best of all, the trains pass through territory that really *looks* like Santa Fe country. The arid, brown landscape features Native American pueblos, a tourist motel on a mesa, even an oil derrick pumping up and down on a hillside next to oil storage tanks.

Surrounding the layout are interactive videos that teach facts about trains and train safety. One video reveals the signal language that engineers and brakemen use to communicate. (The lights convey thirteen different messages; hands deliver seven more.) Another video stresses the need for caution when crossing railroad tracks and the dire consequences for people who dare to drive around lowered crossing gates.

The Railway Gallery also has its share of big trains that kids can watch or climb on. The cutaway cab of the powerful, make-believe Empire State Express is a favorite of kids who want to drive a train. Kids can push a button on the Chicago and Eastern Illinois steam locomotive and see how a steam-powered piston turns the drive wheels of a train. Other full-size engines offer buttons to push and levers to pull to see railway history and physics in action.

A much smaller but slightly more interactive train layout can be found at Berwyn's Toy Trains and Models in Berwyn. While this eight-by-sixteen-foot Lionel train layout runs on automatic, kids can manipulate its accessories—signal lights, crossing gates, and so forth—by pressing buttons outside the layout. Illinois's largest Lionel train dealer, it's a good place to visit if your family is building a layout at home.

Railway Gallery
Museum of Science and Industry
Fifty-seventh Street and Lake Shore Drive
684-1414

Berwyn's Toy Trains and Models
2827 S. Harlem Avenue
Berwyn
(708) 484-4384

Ride-on Trains

From mid-June to early August, preschoolers can power a miniature train with their own steam in Oak Park's Rehm Park. The three-car train fits three pint-size passengers, who propel the train around the track with hand pedals. Staff is on hand in case the train derails or a kid needs help.

The train is open from 1:00 to 4:00 P.M. daily. Lines can be long, but little ones who want to take turn after turn won't mind the wait. While the train is in operation the park is also in full swing, offering supervised arts and crafts, games, and the occasional clown or magician act.

The Rehm Park train is ideal for children who are 3, 4, or 5 years old. Much younger, and they won't be strong enough to make the train move. Any older, and they won't fit!

There is no charge for train rides. Bathrooms and refreshments are available.

Rehm Park
East Avenue and Garfield Avenue
Oak Park
(708) 383-0002

Big Planes

If your child is yearning to take to the wild blue yonder, try a private air tour of Chicago with Tri-Star Pilot Service Tours.

Up to three people can join Captain Jerry Smith on the forty-five-minute tour, which begins at Midway Airport and follows the lakefront to the Bahai Temple and back. Besides pointing out major sights, Captain Smith will answer questions about flying and try to oblige requests to fly over a family's house–although his little Cessna must stay out of the restricted flight paths around Midway and O'Hare Airports.

In Captain Smith's experience, kids love flying in small planes. But they often confuse his Cessna with a Blue Angel, and beg him to try a few spins and rolls. Do your kids a favor and tell them up front that this is a sightseeing trip, not a stunt flight!

You can schedule your tour at your convenience–morning, noon, or night. Many families like to fly at sunset, so they can see Chicago by day as they fly north, and by night as they return to the airport. Either way, be sure to bring your cameras.

Call a week ahead of time to arrange your flight and get directions to the hangar on the south side of Midway Field. Parking is easy, because you'll be nowhere near the main terminal. A forty-five- to sixty-minute tour costs $95 a couple, plus $47.50 a kid.

Tri-Star Pilot Service Tours
Jerry and Jerri Smith
5725 S. Neenah Avenue
229-1091

Watching Planes

Until it closes in 1996, Meigs Field is the best place in town to watch planes roar just a few yards above your head. Walk or drive east from Lake Shore Drive toward the Adler Planetarium on Solidarity Drive to the parking lot at the end of the cul-de-sac. Stand or park in line with the runway, and settle everyone down on the hood for a comfortable—or uncomfortable, depending on how you feel about jets roaring about thirty feet overhead—view of the private jets. The air traffic gets heavy after 3:00 P.M. on weekday afternoons, when corporate honchos return from out-of-town meetings.

For a close look at bigger planes, try Midway Airport. Its three primary flight paths take planes directly over the intersections of Fifty-ninth Street and South Cicero Avenue, Fifty-fifth Street and South Long Avenue, and Sixty-third and South Cicero, where kids can admire planes as they eat sliders in the White Castle parking lot.

Inside the Big Planes

For a look inside a big plane and insights into how hundreds of thousands of pounds of metal get off the ground in the first place, visit the *Take Flight* exhibit at the Museum of Science and Industry.

The major feature, of course, is the Boeing 727, suspended in midair over the Santa Fe Railway layout. Inside the plane, kids can examine the cockpit and instrument panel and eavesdrop on the pilot's conversation. There's a Plexiglas window into the hold, too, so kids can see the equipment under the floor.

Interactive exhibits in the forward cabin greatly simplify the principles of aeronautics and give kids an appreciation of what it takes to navigate a plane. One fascinating activity lets kids guide the plane from Chicago to Buffalo using Instrument Flight Rules. You plot your course by setting the plane's VOR (very-high-frequency omnidirectional radio range) for various stations along the way. Maybe you'll get there, maybe you won't. The computer will let you know!

Most fascinating for kids is a multimedia computer game called The Flying Brick. This clever program lets a child design an aircraft by choosing material (brick, metal, fiberglass, or wood), a shape (square, conical, etc.), wings (single or double), and an engine (propeller or jet). All the major forces—thrust, lift, drag, and weight—are explained before they are manipulated, and a friendly little creature tells kids whether their final product will fly.

Kids can play this game simply by following the very clear commands and touching the monitor. If your kid likes inventing things, plan to hang around the Flying Brick for a while. It lures kids into dreaming up novel new ways to take flight!

Take Flight
Museum of Science and Industry
Fifty-seventh Street and Lake Shore Drive
684-1414

Model Planes and Boats

In our youth, "models" meant small-scale planes and cars assembled from hundreds of plastic pieces with smelly, toxic model glue and paints.

Sure, those models still exist. But far more exciting are the giant model airplanes and boats that cruise Forest Preserve fields and lakes every weekend morning.

Actually, "cruise" isn't quite right. "Blast" is more like it. Model airplanes can reach speeds of 150 miles per hour and heights of hundreds of feet; model boats can race across the water at 100 miles per hour. They're not small, either: boats are generally two to three feet long, and while a typical model airplane is sixty inches long, planes can be as long as nine feet. And they're not quiet. In their quest to be as realistic as possible, model jets and cigarette boats sound just like the real thing!

At the fields and lakes listed below, model boats and planes are operated every Saturday and Sunday morning. (Get there early; most of the action takes place before 10:00 A.M.) Model planes are flown year-round; boating season ends when the lakes freeze over. Don't expect to find these hobbyists out in extremely windy weather (boats can capsize and planes are too hard to control), but you will see planes flown in winter, their landing gear replaced with skis so they can land on snow.

The operators are a friendly bunch, very interested in answering kids' questions about the equipment. Most of them are members of model plane and boat clubs, which are a great source of information and support if your family decides that radio-controlled vehicles is its new hobby!

Model Airplanes

Like their full-sized counterparts, remote-controlled airplanes have a rudder and a throttle, an elevator that controls the altitude, and an aileron that permits the plane to perform rolls and corkscrews. A deft operator can use these instruments to urge his plane into jaw-dropping corkscrews, loops, figure 8s, and rolls. For an eyeful of these fancy maneuvers, head for one of these Forest Preserve fields, set aside for model aircraft:

- George A. Miller Meadow in the Salt Creek Division, east side of First Avenue, a quarter mile north of Cermak Road, adjacent to the I.C. tracks in Maywood

- Kickapoo Woods in the Calumet Division, west side of Halsted Street at 144th Street in Riverdale

- Morrill Meadow in the Palos Division, west side of Mannheim Road, south of 107th Street in Palos Hills

- Ned Brown Preserve in the Northwest Division, south side of Golf Road, east of Interstate 290 in Elk Grove Village

- Schiller Woods in the Indian Boundary Division, south side of Irving Park Road, west of Cumberland Avenue in Chicago

During your visit, you and your kids will have to stay in designated spectator areas. Airplanes do fall out of the sky, and even though most operators are insured and can pay for injuries, it's best to stay out of harm's reach. But your kids can lean over the fence and ask questions about the machines. If you are watching a race, hold questions until after it is over.

Even from the spectator area, your kids will have a great view. Once the planes take off, they operate anywhere from 10 to 500 feet above ground. Most of them fly at about 50 miles per hour, but an acrobatic plane can exceed 100 miles per hour.

Model Boats

The largest and most popular gathering place for model boaters is Lake Ida in the Salt Creek Division of the Forest Preserve District of Cook County. (Lake Ida is near the corner of Sixty-seventh Street and La Grange–Mannheim Road.)

Model boat enthusiasts practice Saturday and Sunday mornings starting at 8:00 A.M. Serious racers get there first, but people bring different kinds of boats all day long. You'll see outboard and inboard motor boats built of wood, plastic, and fiberglass, including model hydroplanes and cigarette boats.

Because there is no designated spectator area, your family can stroll along the shore admiring the vessels. Watch where your kids step, though—some of this equipment costs several hundred dollars!

Model boats are tricky to handle. At minimum, they have a rudder and throttle; some have more sophisticated controls. Many are capable of speeds up to 100 miles per hour, but at all times, the engine must stay dry. That can be tricky during races, when the boats must execute high-speed turns without capsizing. It's tricky, too, in rough weather, even for experienced boaters.

Model boaters also congregate at Pottowatomi Lake in the Des Plaines Division (near Milwaukee Avenue and Dundee Road). Model sailboats can be admired at Axehead Lake in the Indian Boundary Division (Touhy Avenue and Interstate 294), where races are held every other week during the boating season.

The Chicago Model and Hobby Show

Kids who are mad for models shouldn't miss the annual Chicago Model and Hobby Show, held each fall at the O'Hare Expo Center in Rosemont.

In an indoor arena, kids can see demonstrations of gas- and electric-powered model helicopters and planes and operate, under adult supervision, the enormous model train layout. At the thirty-by-sixty-five-foot indoor boat pond, kids can take a turn at the helm of model tug boats, hydroplanes, and other boats. There's even an eight-by-sixteen-foot slot car track, a thirty-five-by-eighty-foot flat track, and a thirty-by-fifty-foot dirt track for model monster trucks.

When kids tire of operating models, they can make them. At make-and-take booths, they can build plastic rockets, airplanes, and train accessories, or participate in lessons on building model railroads of all scales and gauges.

Surrounding the activity area are hundreds of booths where model and hobby companies demonstrate their wares. Take along a bag and load up on samples!

The Chicago Model and Hobby Show is sponsored by the Radio Control Hobby Trade Association and the Model Railroad Industry Association. It is heavily advertised in newspaper inserts the Friday before the weekend show. Watch for information in October, or call the RCHTA at (708) 526-1222 for dates.

9

The Urban Jungle

Dense jungles, humid rain forests, and exotic plants and animals from everywhere are all right here in Chicago, in conservatories, greenhouses, and zoos that make great backdrops for imaginative play and teach essential lessons about the natural world.

Four Indoor Jungles

Forget about icy winds, slippery streets, and heavy coats. On a dead-of-winter expedition to a glass-domed conservatory, your family can enjoy towering palm trees, tangled vines, succulent cacti, and broad paved paths for running, skipping, and games of hide-and-seek—all in a humid, seventy-two-degree environment! Be sure to wear T-shirts under your sweaters so you and your child can savor the novelty of bare arms in winter.

Each of the conservatories offers something different. Garfield Park Conservatory is far and away the biggest and most impressive. Lincoln Park Conservatory is most convenient for northsiders and is easy to pair with a visit to the zoo or another Lincoln Park attraction. The Oak Park Conservatory, the smallest and most intimate, is home to some surprising residents. And the Botanic Garden Greenhouses offer unique learning games that let kids discover how we benefit from plants.

Winter-weary families can also perk up at the seasonal flower shows offered by the Chicago Park District at the Garfield and

Lincoln Park Conservatories. Their uplifting palette of colors includes reds during the December holidays, when giant trees are built from potted poinsettias, pinks and reds during the February Azalea and Camellia Show, and the bright spring colors of tulips, hyacinths, forsythia, primroses, and lilies during the Spring and Easter Show.

Garfield Park Conservatory

The biggest indoor jungle in Chicago really takes your breath away. Under its soaring glass ceilings are four and a half acres of tropical species and surprises, including a fern room that can instantly correct even the worst family case of the no-end-in-sight, long-winter blues.

Because it's on the West Side, the Garfield Park Conservatory doesn't get the visitors it deserves. But if you're driving, there's no need to be intimidated by its Lake Street and Central Park Boulevard location. From the Eisenhower Expressway, exit on Independence Boulevard, go north to Lake Street, and east to the conservatory parking lot. The parking lot is secure, but if you're nervous you can park on the street directly in front of the conservatory.

Inside, everything is warm, cozy, and enormous. The palm trees *really* tower; the mature cactus *really* look like desert residents; and the spectacular central Fern Room is so vast, so lush, and so green that your family will need to rest on the stairs a moment just to take in its brilliance. The conservatory is so big that its flashy contents may overwhelm its scientific message. Your kids probably won't learn much about plants here, but they will surely respond to the imaginative possibilities of a jungle, desert, or tropical paradise under glass. Expect to spend some time pretending you're all explorers on a scientific expedition, or Indiana Jones–style adventurers tracking lost treasure.

The Palm Room and the Fern Room best lend themselves to imaginative play. It's easy to get lost in the Palm Room, and easy to lose yourself in exploring the Fern Room's hidden secrets: ferns growing on rocks, tethered by slim root systems; ferns peeking out of the shadowy recesses of the waterfall; ferns leaning over ponds covered with tropical water lilies and other aquatic plants. There are nooks, crannies, caves, and animals, too, though the conservatory staff does its best to discourage them. Look for squirrels, raccoons, and renegade reptiles, surreptitiously released by people who tire of their pets. One iguana eluded capture for more than two years!

Designed by legendary landscape artist Jens Jensen, the Fern Room can be overlooked if you limit your visit to the path that runs along the building's perimeter. When you've finished exploring the outlying rooms, return to the main room and follow its inner path to the staircase that leads into the Fern Room. Unfortunately, this staircase means that strollers will have to be carried down the steps and the wheelchair-bound may have no choice but to enjoy the view from a distance. (All the other rooms in the conservatory are easy to visit.)

The conservatory is open daily from 9:00 A.M. to 5:00 P.M. During major flower shows, it opens at 10:00 A.M. Admission is free. No snacks are available, but there are bathrooms near the main desk by the entrance.

Garfield Park Conservatory
300 N. Central Park Boulevard
746-5100

Lincoln Park Conservatory

On a winter day, the Lincoln Park Conservatory is still except for the clank of the radiators and the soft murmur of water in the reflecting pond by the front door. A lovely paved path–perfect for strollers or small feet–wends its way among tall palm and fig trees.

When everything outside is white, gray, or brown, this expanse of green is such a relief your family may want to park itself on a bench and soak up the atmosphere. Unlike the Garfield Park Conservatory, which is a little short on benches, in this conservatory there's always a spot to sit and admire the palette of greens or the splash of color of a seasonal flower show.

The Lincoln Park Conservatory is much smaller than the Garfield Park Conservatory, but it still offers plenty for your kids to see: real bananas growing on a banana tree, goldfish swimming in lagoons, and a desert garden with cacti in many interesting shapes. Your family can see all the rooms of the conservatory quickly, but if it's winter, you'll probably want to linger.

The Lincoln Park Conservatory is open daily from 10:00 A.M. to 5:00 P.M. Bathrooms are just inside the front door; free parking is available outside on Stockton Drive.

Lincoln Park Conservatory
2400 N. Stockton Drive
742-7736

Oak Park Conservatory

This cozy little conservatory is the perfect size for young children who feel dwarfed by the Garfield or Lincoln Park Conservatories. It's also home to a delightful collection of birds, fish, and reptiles that will charm the 6-and-under set.

Its narrow paths meander through a desert house, a fern house, and a tropic house, where a little bridge crosses a double lagoon and a waterfall cascades down a wall. Because all the plants are in raised beds, little children can come practically eye-to-eye with coffee and papaya plants, prickly pear cactus, and birds-of-paradise.

They can enjoy the antics of real birds, too. In the Fern House, two large flight cages are home to colorful, talkative cockatiels and parakeets. In the Tropic House, the African gray parrot, Larry Bird, whistles, says hello, and meows like a cat. A birdsong sound track adds a nice jungley touch to the atmosphere. Let your little kids look for the other residents of the Tropic House pond: a painted turtle, a snapping turtle, and brightly colored goldfish, fantails, and koi. And don't overlook the Curiosity Corner, where kids can get their hands on plants with different textures and scents. There are even easy-to-propagate plants that kids can transplant and take home.

The Oak Park Conservatory is open every day of the year from 10:00 A.M. to 4:00 P.M. except Monday, when it is open from 2:00 to 4:00 P.M. Admission is free, but donations are gladly accepted. Most of the conservatory is wheelchair accessible, but you will have to call first to make arrangements to enter through the rear. Bathrooms are available by request, but are not handicapped accessible.

Because this conservatory is small, half an hour is plenty of time to see everything it holds. To make an afternoon of it, cross East Avenue and visit the tiny train, swing sets, and jungle gyms of Rehm Park. During the summer, you can visit the conservatory, play on the swing set, and swim at the Rehm Pool ([708] 848-2929), which has a toddler wading pool, a diving well with three diving boards, and an Olympic-sized pool. A nonresident day pass costs $4.

Oak Park Conservatory
615 Garfield Street
Oak Park
(708) 386-4700

Chicago Botanic Garden Greenhouses

With 10,000 square feet under glass, the Botanic Garden greenhouses fall somewhere between the Lincoln Park and Oak Park Conservatories in size. But when it comes to interpreting its collection, it leads the pack.

Like the conservatories, the Botanic Garden has an arid greenhouse full of cacti and other succulents, and a large, humid tropical room full of "economic" plants. The Botanic Garden does a fantastic job helping kids understand that these plants yield fruit, timber, oil, perfume, spices, and medications used by humans. Kids can pick up a basket of items like cinnamon sticks, comb fibers, and coffee beans, and then search the greenhouse for the plant whose color code matches the item.

A safari to the east greenhouse brings kids face-to-face with a wonderful menagerie of topiary shaped like animals. There's an

Families enjoy nature-related crafts in the cozy interior of the green-houses at the Chicago Botanic Garden. *Courtesy the Chicago Botanic Garden.*

orangutan, a toucan, a very large elk, a donkey, a camel, a flamingo, and even a scarecrow. This is not just a collection of neatly trimmed ivy. Each animal has been created from plants and plant material that resemble the animal's characteristics. So the flamingo is made of pink plants, and the orangutan's spiny-leaved plants are hairlike.

Kids also like the terrariums of the ferocious Venus's-flytrap, pitcher plant, and other carnivorous plants. For water lovers, there's a geometric waterfall and two 150-gallon aquariums. One shows tropical aquatic fish and plants, the other displays fish and plants native to Illinois.

The greenhouses are connected by a hallway with tables that make a nice spot for a picnic. During the winter, the hallway is also the sight of many weekend family workshops, like a topiary safari that introduces kids to the topiary collection.

The Chicago Botanic Garden is open every day except Christmas from 8:00 A.M. to sunset. The greenhouses are attached to the Education Center, which is wheelchair accessible and has plenty of bathrooms. Admission is free and parking is $4 a car.

Chicago Botanic Garden
1000 Lake Cook Road
Glencoe
(708) 835-5440

Brookfield Zoo

Forget about trying to see Brookfield Zoo in one day. With 215 acres and nearly 3,000 animal residents in twenty-four major animal exhibits, Brookfield is the king of the jungle—a destination to return to again and again.

Each of its animal exhibits hosts a fascinating mix of species in a dramatic setting that tries to be accurate down to the tiniest detail. Signs of human life incorporated into each exhibit draw children's attention to information about the animals and their habitat. In the Fragile Desert, for example, scarves dropped by a passing caravan mark "clues," revealing secrets of the desert's rich life.

Because the zoo is so spacious, its naturalistic mixed species exhibits are large. Habitat Africa!, which highlights Africa's diverse wildlife and habitats, covers five acres. Set in a mythical African reserve called Makundi National Park, it features two unique landscapes: a rocky outcrop called a kopje, and a water hole where animals gather for nourishment. In the indoor and outdoor kopje, kids can see dwarf mongooses, tortoises, lizards, birds, and even African wild dogs who roam the outcrop, coming nose to nose with young visitors through the glass viewing bays. The water hole area is visited by hoofed animals like giraffes, zebras, antelopes, and ostriches.

A researcher's jeep full of materials confiscated from poachers impresses upon kids that poaching is a threat to many species. Instead of presenting conservation information on a static sign, facts and caveats blare from the jeep's two-way radio and the radio in the Makundi National Park office near the water hole.

Don't miss the Thirsty Animal Trail, a hidden, winding footpath that invites kids to find the water source—the Thirsty Animal Drinking Fountain—without becoming someone's meal!

Among the zoo's other imaginative and exciting exhibits is the Fragile Desert, a replica of a desert in North Africa, where children can explore lots of small nooks and crannies and search for the clues (marked by a dropped scarf) that explain the secrets of this fascinating habitat. (On a hot day, the Fragile Desert is deliciously dark and cool—a great escape from an enervating afternoon.)

For a cool treat on a hot day, or a lush, tropical respite during the middle of a snowstorm, visit the zoo's two rain forests. Tropic World, one of the world's largest indoor zoo exhibits, represents the rain forest regions of South America, Asia, and Africa. To view its 140 animal residents, kids follow a pathway that overlooks pools, waterfalls, and enormous trees that make up the animals' jungle home. Try to visit Tropic World during one of its hourly thunderstorms, when thunder and lightning crash but only the animals get wet.

The second, smaller rain forest is inside the Fragile Kingdom building. Small jungle animals cavort in this Asian rain forest, painstakingly crafted to include a researcher's cabin and chalkboard marked with field notes. Besides giving you the feeling that you're a million miles from Chicago, both rain forests are full of kid surprises: animals lurking in trees, swinging or leaping between trees, hiding behind bushes, or enjoying a snack.

The zoo's dolphinarium, the Seven Seas Panorama, seats 2,000 people for its thrilling water shows. You'll pay extra to see the dolphins frolic—unless you take your family to the lower level and watch the underwater half of the show. Watching the dolphins swim up, up, and up, vanish altogether for an instant, and then plunge back into the pool in a majestic fountain of bubbles is a truly exciting—and cheap!—thrill for kids. Outside the dolphinarium you can admire the larger marine animals: walruses, seals, and sea lions.

Listing each of the zoo's exhibits would take another ten pages. Rest assured that no matter what exhibit your family chooses to visit, your kids will love it.

Keep in mind, however, that the Brookfield Zoo is a huge place, and you will all get tired. The good news is that the zoo offers many amenities that will help you prevent family meltdown. The bad news is that many of them cost money. (Don't worry about running out of cash—there's even an ATM here.) Bathrooms are free (find them with the zoo's great map), but restaurants, food carts, ice cream, and souvenirs are not.

Neither is the forty-five-minute guided Motor Safari around the zoo, but in this case, your money may be well spent. The safari makes four stops, so you can reach some of the zoo's far-flung exhibits while minimizing kid complaints about sore feet. Weather permitting, the Motor Safari runs from early spring through late fall. Adults cost $3, kids under 11 and seniors over 65 cost $1, and children under 3 are free.

Workshops and Tours

The zoo's busy Education Department sponsors many weekend and weekday programs for children of all ages. Preschoolers meet for simple games and learning experiences; older kids can enjoy more in-depth classes on specific animals, habitats, and scientific careers.

A perennial favorite for kids and parents is Backstage at the Zoo. Open to anyone over the age of 8, the early morning tours offer a buffet breakfast before exploring an animal exhibit, meeting its keeper, and learning more about specific animals, their adaptations, and their care.

These behind-the-scenes tours visit more than ten animal areas. The most popular (and most frequently offered) visit is Habitat Africa! and the Big Cats, where families can get awfully close to the cat holding area and are often treated to a roaring ruckus. Offered only once a quarter but very, very popular is Feasts for Beasts, a tour of the commissary where animal meals are prepared. Tours are offered Saturday and Sunday mornings every season but summer. Breakfast is at 8:30 A.M., and the hour-long tour starts at 9:30 A.M. Saturday and Sunday mornings. For members, tickets are $20 an adult, $11 a child; nonmembers pay $23 and $14, respectively. (For more behind-the-scenes tours, see chapter 14, "Chicago Behind the Scenes.")

Summer zoo camp is offered to kids in four different age groups: 3 to 5 years, kindergarten and first grade, second and third grade, and fourth through sixth grade. Little kids focus on what it means to be an animal, examining how animals move, where they live, what they eat, and what their families are like. Older kids might study various animal habitats or the adaptations of aardvarks, platypuses, and other unusual animals in the zoo's collection.

The weeklong camps, which run from 9:30 A.M. to 1:00 P.M., fill up quickly, even though each one is offered two to five times during the summer. Call the Education Department in the spring for the camp preview brochure, and plan to sign your child up early. Camps cost between $80 and $115 and include a T-shirt, daily snacks, five days of great fun, and a Friday open house where parents can see what their kids have been up to.

The Brookfield Zoo also offers a wonderful family overnight, Wild Night Overnight. Details are in chapter 13.

To find out more about Brookfield Zoo workshops, tours, and special events, ask the Education Department to send you its seasonal calendar. (Join the zoo, and you'll be notified first— long before the 50,000 other people who receive the catalog!) Preregistration is required for these programs.

The Brookfield Zoo is open daily from 10:00 A.M. to 4:30 P.M. Its extended daily summer hours are 9:30 A.M. to 5:00 P.M. Admission is $4 for adults and $1.50 for kids under 11 and seniors over 65. On Tuesdays and Thursdays from April through September, admission rates are reduced to $2 and $.75, respectively. From October to March, admission is free on Tuesdays and Thursdays. It costs an additional $4 to park your car.

Brookfield Zoo
First Avenue and Thirty-first Street
Brookfield
General information: (708) 485-0263
Education Department: extension 361

Lincoln Park Zoo

Are your kids ready to tangle with the urban jungle's fiercest creatures? Then plan an expedition to the Lincoln Park Zoo, home to more than 1,000 species of animals from all around the world.

The zoo is a wonderful place to spend an afternoon. Because it's smack in the middle of Lincoln Park, you can bookend your zoo trip with a stroll in the park, a horse-and-carriage ride, or a paddleboat trip. (See chapter 11, "More Great Outdoors," for details on Lincoln Park amenities.)

Children of all ages can enjoy a visit to the zoo. Very young children can feel a small mammal's soft fur, or get their first eyeful of elephant. Older children can absorb more detailed information about animal habitats and behaviors through the zoo's informative signage at traveling Curiosity Carts.

Part of the zoo's mission is to teach kids about the importance of preserving our environment and all its wildlife. Whether kids visit the mighty predators in the Kovler Lion House, watch the social interactions of the gorillas in the Fisher Great Ape House, or laugh at the antics of the seals and sea lions, they'll be learning lessons about animal conservation—lessons all dressed up as family fun.

Many lessons can be learned at the traveling Curiosity Carts, loaded with "biofacts" or biological specimens and staffed by docents who can answer questions. The Curiosity Cart that visits the Reptile House gives kids a chance to handle skins, skeletons, shells, and skulls. In the McCormick Bird House, the cart features bird nests, eggs, and feathers. The Tools of the Trade Cart lets kids touch the equipment many zookeepers use to care for their charges.

During the informal Wildlife Encounters scheduled throughout the day, kids can learn more about a particular way an animal has adapted to its environment. A docent might bring along a giraffe neck bone to show how the world's tallest mammal can comfortably nibble from branches twenty feet above the ground, or a bear's skull to illustrate how formidable even a plant-eating bear's teeth can be.

There are also plenty of chances to watch animals being fed and examined. With elephants using their trunks to eat and apes casually dropping carrot stubs on the floor, meals at the zoo probably resemble meals at your place. During the summer kids can get a taste of their own manners when the apes, sea lions, and seals are fed from 2:00 to 3:00 P.M.

Kids can see elephant keepers at work during the Elephant Workout, held daily at 1:30 P.M. at the elephant habitat. To keep the elephants healthy, keepers check these giants' teeth, skin, and foot pads.

The Pritzker Children's Zoo

At the Pritzker Children's Zoo, a young child can touch an iguana or learn about an animal's life and home. Every day from 10:00 A.M. to 2:00 P.M., the Children's Zoo offers short, kid-focused presentations on zoo babies, animal diets, and animal adaptation, along with ample opportunities for kids to touch various furry, scaly, or feathered friends.

Surrounding the Children's Zoo are the outdoor gardens, where white-tailed deer, woodchucks, river otters, porcupines, and other native Illinois wildlife make their homes. Kids can scan the area for animal homes and hiding places above, below, and on the ground.

Inside the Children's Zoo during program hours, volunteers offer kids the chance to get close to an animal. It may be touchable, like a guinea pig or turtle, or one that kids want to examine closely without touching, like a parrot or a hermit crab.

Three specially designed Curiosity Carts let kids learn more about the animal world. The Zookeeper Cart displays tools zookeepers use to give an elephant a pedicure or to move a snake. Using rubber stamps of different animal feet, the Feet First Cart helps kids learn how feet, flippers, and claws enable animals to walk, swim, or perch on a limb. The Animal Lunchbox Cart, generally around during lunch hour, answers questions about what animals eat and why. Lunchtime is also a good time to watch zookeepers prepare dishes for residents in the Children's Zoo kitchen. The chefs helpfully post recipe cards showing what each animal is about to enjoy!

Because every kid loves baby animals, the nursery inside the Children's Zoo is a wonderful place to see animals that need to be raised by hand. But zoo staff likes it empty, because an empty nursery means the zoo's animals are raising their own babies. There's plenty to learn about baby animals even when the nursery is empty. Children's Zoo volunteers frequently talk about the care of young animals and show how zookeepers adapt bottles, nipples, and other equipment to feed injured, sick, or motherless infants.

While most Children's Zoo activities are geared to the under-6 set, the Conservation Station teaches older kids basic lessons in conservation and science while encouraging them to take a stand on environmental issues. Through fun, hands-on activities, kids can learn about topics like wetlands development and recycling, and find out how to pass along their thoughts to elected officials.

If you're planning a visit, call the zoo first to find out what's scheduled at the Children's Zoo. Programs hours are extended summer months.

Family Workshops and Field Trips

Families with children over 6 can often make animal masks and marionettes, meet a pteranodon, or enjoy behind-the-scenes tours of the animal houses, thanks to the zoo's appealing workshops, field trips, and camps. The zoo even hosts performing groups like the Banana Slug String Band, a group of California science teachers who wrote the kid hit, "Dirt Made My Lunch."

Held fall, winter, and spring weekends, ninety-minute Wildlife Workshops study a specific group of animals and their behavior. The workshop on Primate Family Trees, for example, invites kids to compare hand- and footprints of different primates, find out why people are primates, and make a family tree to take home. They take a guided tour of the Helen Brach Primate House, and meet a zookeeper who helps care for these intelligent creatures.

Similar programs introduce kids to bears, boas, giraffes, and their keepers, or take them on a visit to the Kroc Zoo Hospital where they can meet its attending veterinarians.

In its role as champion of endangered animals and habitats, the zoo sponsors several fascinating field trips that help urban families understand more about our own habitat. One popular trip visits Cozzi Iron and Metal, Inc., a steel-recycling firm that processes 120,000 autos a year in Chicago alone. Kids 9 and over who love heavy machinery will marvel at the sight of cars being shredded in mere seconds. The resulting small bits of steel are used in new products, closing the "loop" in the recycling cycle and vividly demonstrating how a family's recycling habits affect our home.

Another fascinating trip introduces adults and teens 14 and older to the canine enforcement officers and dogs who work the O'Hare Airport Customs beat. Besides getting a behind-the-scenes look at the customs operation, you'll learn about the tactics smugglers use to try to bring drugs into the country, and how customs relies on animals to thwart these efforts.

Zoo field trips are always changing; check the seasonal catalog to find out what is being offered and who can go.

During the dog days of summer, Zoo Camps immerse kids 5 through 12 in topics like wildlife habitats and animal adaptation. Field trips, behind-the-scenes tours, crafts and projects, hikes and snacks fill these weeklong camps. Subjects change every summer, so budding zoologists can attend year after year after year and never hear the same thing twice.

To find out about the zoo's family overnights, workshops, camps, and field trips, call the Education Department and ask to be sent the current season's catalog. You can be added to the permanent mailing list after you attend a program.

The Lincoln Park Zoo is easy on walkers. Paths are wide and exhibits are contained within a thirty-five-acre area. All exhibits are stroller and wheelchair accessible. Strollers and wagons can be rented from 10:00 A.M. to 4:00 P.M. just east of the Landmark Cafe; wheelchairs are available at no charge during the same hours at the Lion House Information Center.

The zoo is open every day of the year from 9:00 A.M. to 5:00 P.M., free of charge. (Parking on Cannon Drive costs $3.) During field trip seasons in May and October, the zoo can be crowded and the parking area clogged with school buses loading and unloading kids. If you want to avoid big groups, visit after 1:00 P.M. During winter months your family will have the zoo practically to itself!

Food is available year-round at Cafe Brauer, which serves salads, sandwiches, pizza, and burgers. (Kid's meals are packaged in an attractive animal bag and include a toy.) During warm weather there are more dining options: several food carts on the zoo's main mall, the Elephant Cafe near the outdoor elephant habitat (Italian beef sandwiches, chicken wings, sandwiches and snacks), and the Landmark Cafe across from the Sea Lion Pool (hot dogs, etc.). Ice cream, yogurt, cappuccino, and espresso are available at the Cafe Brauer Ice Cream Shop, open during the summer until 10:00 P.M.

Lincoln Park Zoo
2200 N. Cannon Drive
Education Department: 742-7692
General information: 935-6700
Recorded information: 742-7696

Lincoln Park Zoo's Farm-in-the-Zoo

Does your city child know that milk comes from cows, eggs from chickens, and bacon from pigs? At the Farm-in-the-Zoo, kids can watch cows being milked and sheep being sheared, or see a chick hatch from its shell. While feeding, milking, and grooming schedules vary from season to season, there is always something happening between 10:00 A.M. and 2:00 P.M.

Each farm building is home to a different kind of domestic animal. Powerful Clydesdales and cute Shetland ponies live in the Horse Barn, where kids can learn how horses have helped build civilization through their contributions to agriculture and transportation.

In the Dairy Barn kids can help feed a cow, watch it being milked, and then check a computer screen to see how much milk it produced. Cows are milked at 10:00 A.M., noon, and 2:00 P.M.; butter is churned at 10:00 A.M. on weekdays, 1:00 P.M. on weekends.

Inside the Poultry Barn are elegant breeds of hens and roosters and an incubator full of tiny chicks pecking their way out of their shells. Kids can meet the young chicks during Meet the Animals, when sheep, chicks, and goats are brought into the yard or inside the Main Barn's demonstration area for petting and close inspection.

Even kids who hate going to the doctor enjoy a chance to peek into a veterinarian's bag, one of several activities in the Harness on Health animal-care demonstration. Kids are always amazed to see the enormous hypodermic needles used to pierce tough animal hides, and the oversize pills prescribed for cows. The Farm-in-the-Zoo works hard to make sure children appreciate how much of their everyday life is affected by agriculture. Besides displays on ancient and recent agricultural history, workshops like Back to the Farm let kids match items like cheese, eggs, lipstick, and glue to the animals and plants that produced them. Mom and Dad will appreciate Food for Thought, which offers basic nutritional information needed to make wise food choices.

Located just south of the main zoo, the Farm-in-the-Zoo is open every day from 9:00 A.M. to 4:30 P.M. Admission to all buildings is free.

Lincoln Park Zoo's Farm-in-the-Zoo
1801 N. Stockton Drive
742-7692

A Teeny Tiny Little Zoo

It doesn't offer any programs or special activities, but Indian Boundary Zoo in Indian Boundary Park lets children get close to smaller animals like goats, llamas, and raccoons. The birds and mammals who live here are all hardy species adapted to cold-weather climates. Weather permitting, your child can touch and stroke them in the petting pen, open daily from 10:00 to 11:30 A.M. and from 1:00 to 2:30 P.M.

Indian Boundary Zoo sits right next to the spectacular Indian Boundary Playground, an irresistible collection of turrets and staircases, bridges, teepees, and tunnels. On a warm afternoon, buy ice-cream cones from Baskin-Robbins at the corner of Lunt Street and Western Avenue, and enjoy them as you sit by the lovely duck pond.

The Indian Boundary Zoo is open daily from 9:00 A.M. to 4:00 P.M. If you plan to bring a very large group of children with you, call the Indian Boundary Park Fieldhouse (742-7887) to make arrangements.

Indian Boundary Zoo
2500 W. Lunt Street
742-7862

10

Urbs in
the Forest
The Forest Preserve District of
Cook County

When you and your kids are tired of city streets and city parks, why not visit the forests, fields, and country lanes of our very own forest preserves?

Eleven percent of the land in Cook County is owned and managed by the Forest Preserve District for the enjoyment of Cook County residents. Its 67,700 acres comprise eleven divisions that run from far northwest Barrington to far southeast Sauk Village and offer literally hundreds of wonderful activities—almost all of them completely free—to you and your children. Its vast holdings include:

- 200 miles of trails for hiking and horseback riding

- More than 75 miles of paved bike trails

- 36 lakes, ponds, and sloughs managed for fishing

- 87 miles of shoreline

- Dozens of cross-country ski trails

- A Nordic ski school certified by the PSIA, Professional Ski Instructors of America

- 14 toboggan slides at five locations

- 9 model airplane fields

- 2 lakes for model watercraft

- 6 nature and environmental education centers, offering seasonal programs for the entire family

- 4,400 acres of nature preserves

- 4 lakes where sailboats, rowboats, and canoes can be rented

In spite of these riches, the Forest Preserve District doesn't often come to mind when city residents think of activities for children. Maybe it's because people associate the Forest Preserves with the suburbs instead of the city. Maybe it's because we get so involved in our urban lives that we forget to stop and smell the flowers. Whatever the reason, think "Forest Preserve" for outdoor family adventures and start gathering the tools needed to navigate and enjoy these jewels of Cook County.

Getting to Know the Forest Preserve District

A single call to Forest Preserve District headquarters in River Forest will net you a wealth of brochures, maps, and calendars of year-round family fun. Ask for a map of recreational facilities, which shows all of the Forest Preserve holdings and lists every resource within its boundaries, including picnic areas, fishing lakes and ponds, bicycle trails, toboggan slides, golf courses, and swimming pools.

In the same call (or after you have studied the map and identified the holdings closest to you) you can request maps of picnic areas and trails for each of the District's eleven divisions.

These maps will help you plot walks and cycling tours through forests, meadows, and prairies. They'll also help you find amenities in a particular park, such as the snowmobile area in Ned Brown Preserve or the toboggan slides in Palos Preserve. And they'll tell you about each preserve's geological and social history, botanical highlights, and points of interest.

The points of interest alone will give you plenty of ideas for excursions. How about a visit to a stop on the Underground Railway in the Thorn Creek Division? Or to Powderhorn Lake in the Calumet Division, where prickly pear cactus grows in abundance along the sandy shores? Or landlocked Mount Forest Island in the Palos Preserve, which once jutted out from prehistoric Lake Chicago?

If you're interested in a particular activity such as fishing or cross-country skiing, the Forest Preserve publishes specific brochures in these areas:

- A fishing guide that contains depth contours for the major lakes, tells what kind of fish are stocked, and the catch size limit

- A winter guide tells where winter sports activities—skiing, sledding, ice-skating, ice fishing, and snowmobiling—take place in the District (for more information, see chapter 12, "Winter Wonderland")

- Maps of each of the 8 designated bicycle trails

- Cross-country ski trail maps for each division

- Bird and wildlife checklists

- Portage canoe trail map

There is also a monthly calendar that offers an enticing menu of free special events. For the month of October alone, for example, your kids can enjoy a splishy-splashy hike through Cook County's only rock canyon, a spooky night hike through the forest in Palos Preserve, a cozy fireside nature chat around a campfire at Sand Ridge Nature Center, an exciting fossil hunt through Sagawau Division quarries, a fall color walk-through at the Trailside Museum in River Forest, a spine-tingling visit to the Haunted Forest at Caldwell Woods, and a nature story time for toddlers at River Trail Nature Center in Northbrook.

Once these helpful brochures are in your possession, convene a family meeting to decide where to begin your adventures in the Forest Preserve District.

Forest Preserve District of Cook County
General Headquarters
536 North Harlem Avenue
River Forest
There are four numbers you can call for maps and information on trails, summer or winter sports, and outdoor recreation and nature programs in the Forest Preserve:
261-8400
(708) 366-9420
(800) 870-3666
TDD: (708) 771-1190
For picnic permits and more detailed information about golf courses, ice-skating, ice-fishing, and toboggan slides, call the Recreation Department.

For general information about nature education programs, ask for the Conservation Department.

● ●

Forest Preserve District of Cook County Publications:

- Bicycle Trail Maps

- Bird and Wildlife Checklists

- Cross-Country Ski Trail Maps

- Fishing Guide

- Picnic Area and Trail Maps

- Portage Canoe Trail Map
- Recreational Facilities Map
- Winter Guide

● ●

Hiking and Biking on
Forest Preserve District Trails

When you use a Forest Preserve District trail, you'll be sharing it with hikers, mountain bikers, runners, horseback riders, and in the winter, skiers.

While many recreation districts are moving away from multiuse trails and designating trails for single uses such as mountain biking or hiking, the Forest Preserve District strives to keep trails open to all. To that end it sponsors trail etiquette courses and prints trail rules on the back of its maps. On all trails, bicyclists are to keep to the right of the trail and alert anyone they are about to overtake. Ride single file, and don't go faster than eight miles per hour. Just like streets and highways, the trails are monitored by radar, and speeding bicyclists will be ticketed. To prevent collisions, walkers and joggers should use the left side facing oncoming bicycle traffic.

The picnic areas and trail maps of each division clearly indicate footpaths, developed trails, and paved bicycle trails in each division. Maps that indicate parking, areas of interest, and rest stops for tired kids are also available for these bike trails:

- Arie Crown Forest Preserve in Countryside (3.2 miles)

- Busse Woods in Arlington Heights (11.2 miles)

- Deer Grove in Palatine (3.9 miles)

- I & M Canal in Willow Springs (8.9 miles)

- North Branch in Chicago (20 miles)

- Thorn Creek in Park Forest (2.5 miles)

128 ••• KIDS IN THE LOOP •••

- Tinley Creek in Palos Heights (3.2 miles)
- Salt Creek in North Riverside (6.6 miles)

The North Branch is the longest, most popular, and often most crowded. Starting in Chicago's Caldwell Woods, it wends its way past the Skokie Lagoons and the Chicago Botanic Garden on its way to Lake County. Some riders continue northward all the way to Wisconsin! If you are riding with several children, or with a child who is just learning the rules of the road, you might start off with a less-crowded trail, or ride this one on weekdays only. Congestion at Deer Grove and Busse Woods makes these trails difficult for beginners, too.

Forest Preserve Nature Centers

Forest Preserve District nature centers can help your kids get to know the hundreds of species of animals and plants that dwell in the region. By day, the centers' knowledgeable staffers lead nature walks and programs about the world of spring wildflowers, frogs and toads, the marsh environment, and many other fascinating habitats. By night, naturalists lead night hikes in which children use their hearing to discover nocturnal creatures, and astronomers sponsor star watches that explore the glories of the night sky.

A nature center visit is rewarding even when no special programming is scheduled. Your kids can "ooh" and "aah" over its animals, ramble along its paved trails, poke around in mud with sticks, or look for wildlife. Signs along the trails alert kids to points of interest such as natural wetlands, rare wildflowers, or bird nests. Bathrooms are available at each nature center, but not along the trails, which are from a quarter mile to a mile in length.

Each of these centers publishes a seasonal activity schedule that you can pick up at the center or request from Forest Preserve District headquarters. Get a copy so you don't miss any of the excitement!

All Forest Preserve nature centers have the same hours. From March through October, nature center areas are open weekdays from 8:00 A.M. to 5:00 P.M., and weekends until 5:30 P.M. The nature center buildings are open Monday through Thursday from 9:00 A.M. to 4:30 P.M., and weekends until 5:00 P.M. All nature center buildings are closed on Fridays, but the grounds stay open, so you can wander along the trails.

From November through February, nature center areas close at 4:30 P.M. and buildings close at 4:00 P.M. Nature centers are closed on Thanksgiving, Christmas, and New Year's Day.

Crabtree Nature Center

The exhibits in this interpretive facility focus on the natural history of surrounding forests, wetlands, and tallgrass prairie. The center also houses a few small animals, a weather station, and a public reading room of nature periodicals and bulletins.

If your child is interested in the prairie, be sure to see Crabtree's impressive eighty acres of restored tallgrass prairie. A highlight of the center's numerous family programs is the Fire of Autumn, which examines the reasons Native Americans set fire to the prairie at the end of each growing season.

In the spring, Crabtree offers an abundance of programs on bird migration. Outdoor stations identify species and explain the significance of migration patterns, while viewing stations in different habitats provide a secluded spot for children to spy on migrating birds.

Crabtree Nature Center
Route 3, Stover Road
Barrington
(708) 381-6592

Little Red Schoolhouse

Built in 1886, this former schoolhouse on the shores of Long John Slough is one of the most popular nature centers in the Forest Preserve District. Start your visit inside the schoolhouse, where kids can admire fish, snapping turtles, a raccoon, and a bullfrog whose gorgeous gold-flecked eyes are the size of marbles. Outside, there's a pump that really works, and a farm equipment exhibit that explains the history of farms in Cook County.

Paved stroller- and wheelchair-accessible trails take you through the forest and around the slough, where kids can watch for turtles, fish, and other wildlife. Observation blinds along the water's edge offer a fun hideout and a great spot for spying the antics of the local bird population.

The Little Red Schoolhouse's nature programs run the gamut from a slide presentation on the ecology and history of the Palos and Sag Preserves to night hikes, early morning bird walks, and lectures on helping orphaned wildlife.

Little Red Schoolhouse
9900 S. Willow Springs Road
(104th Avenue south of 95th Street)
Willow Springs
(708) 839-6897

River Trail Nature Center

River Trail Nature Center is in a beautiful stretch of sugar maple forest along the Des Plaines River. In addition to seasonal nature programs for children and families, the nature center features an herb garden, a honeybee colony, orchard, and three self-guiding, half-mile nature trails.

Drop by River Trail during one of its two big celebrations: the March Sugar Maple Festival, and the October Honey and Harvest Festival. (For details, see chapter 17, "Powwows, Parties, and Parades.")

River Trail Nature Center
3120 Milwaukee Avenue
(a quarter mile southeast of River Road)
Northbrook
(708) 824-8360

Sand Ridge Nature Center

Sand Ridge Nature Center in South Holland offers family programs every Saturday at 1:30 P.M. At Sand Ridge, you can also enjoy monthly nature story hours, evening skits by the campfire, night hikes through the forest, and daylight walks through wetlands, marshes, and the center's tallgrass prairie.

A collection of small log cabins, replicas of those built by settlers in the mid-nineteenth century, is the site of weekly demonstrations on pioneer life. Wednesday mornings from May through November, volunteers clad in period costume demonstrate crafts like spinning yarn, dipping candles, and making soap and jelly. In very hot weather, when candles won't dry, the volunteers weave baskets instead. Preregistration is not necessary for the demonstrations, which run from 10:00 A.M. to noon.

Inside the nature center is an exhibit room displaying animals and insects, and a cozy Kid's Corner where children can examine animal skulls, do puzzles, draw, and color. All Sand Ridge facilities are stroller and wheelchair accessible.

Sand Ridge Nature Center
15890 Paxton Avenue
South Holland
(708) 868-0606

Trailside Museum

The Trailside Museum is Cook County's official animal rehabilitation center. It accepts nearly 3,000 injured or orphaned wild animals a year, nursing them back to health and releasing into the wild those that can function. (If you happen to find a critter in your yard, you can bring it to the center or call to find someone to come and pick it up.)

Housed outside and inside the museum are owls, a gray fox, crows, and other native wild animals that can no longer survive in the wild. (Off-limits to visitors are animals who are recuperating, because in order to be released, their interactions with people must be limited.) The naturalist on duty will tell your children all about the animals, where they should be living, and how they got to the museum.

A strong conservation theme runs through Trailside's special programs and workshops. Because their goal is to save animals, naturalists take care to explain why, as open land is developed and animals lose their homes, negative encounters between animals and people increase, and animals are hurt. Your children will get a firsthand lesson in the consequences of human behavior for the animal kingdom.

Trailside Museum
738 Thatcher Avenue
Chicago Avenue and Thatcher Avenue
River Forest
(708) 366-6530

Camp Sagawau

Camp Sagawau is an environmental education center open for scheduled programs and for naturalist-conducted tours of Cook County's only rock canyon, Sagawau Canyon Nature Preserve.

Camp Sagawau's programs include walks and hikes through the camp's woods and prairie, and guided tours of nearby wonders like McClaughry Springs and the Cap Sauers State Nature Preserve. Its family programs are imaginative and lots of fun. Who can resist a program like Animal Tracks, in which kids identify and preserve tracks of native animals by making plaster casts?

In the winter Camp Sagawau operates a cross-country ski school where you and your family can rent equipment and learn to ski. (See chapter 12, "Winter Wonderland," for details.)

A Hike Through Sagawau Canyon

Did you know that 410 million years ago, during the Silurian era, before the continents broke apart and drifted to their present-day positions, Illinois was more or less where Brazil is today?

A fascinating remnant of that era is Sagawau Canyon, a twenty-foot-deep, half-mile-long limestone canyon that runs through Camp Sawagau. Once a coral reef, the canyon is filled with fossils and rare plants and may only be visited in the company of a naturalist.

Canyon hikes are held once a week from April through July, and in October. This is a splishy-splashy, get-wet kind of adventure that is a little rough for kids under 4 and is off-limits to anyone in a stroller. (Don't try it with a Snugli either.) To spare the canyon's fragile habitat, visitors march down the middle of the creek. The naturalists wear big rubber waders; your kids should, too.

Before you hike the canyon, call and ask about the water level. Early spring runoff can make the April and May hikes awfully deep, wet, and cold. Tranquil water makes the July and October hikes safer for young children. In very tricky spots, all the explorers hold hands to keep their balance on slippery rocks and in deep pools.

As you walk along the creek, the naturalist helps you and your kids find fossils, animal skeletons, poison ivy (wear long pants!) and its natural antidote, the jewel plant, and other fascinating flora and fauna unique to the canyon. Your whole family will enjoy hearing about prehistoric Illinois, and how today's Chicago area was created by Ice Age glaciers.

Betcha didn't know that a continental divide runs along Archer Avenue. Rain that falls to its north flows to the Atlantic Ocean via the Great Lakes and the St. Lawrence River. Rain that falls to its south flows to the Mississippi River and empties into the Gulf of Mexico. That's just one of the fabulous facts your kids will pick up during this expedition! (Another little-known fact is that Sagawau Canyon was the model for the canyon on display at the Chicago Academy of Sciences.)

When the canyon narrows into a waterfall that spills into a pool too deep to ford, you exit by climbing a natural staircase along the canyon's wall, and can stroll *en famille* through the rest of the prairies and forests of Camp Sagawau.

Wear your boots for a hike through Sagawau Canyon. You and your kids will wade down the middle of the creek as you search for signs of life from 300,000 years ago. *Photo by Michael T. Konrath.*

Searching for Fossils

Take your young paleontologists on a bona fide fossil hunt, and let them take home their finds!

Sponsored by Camp Sagawau, this adventure starts in a quarry on the north side of Route 83 one mile east of Archer Avenue. Look for a yellow Forest Preserve truck displaying the sign, Fossil Hunt. After a geological orientation to the area and a show-and-tell of the kind of fossils children can expect to find, you and your kids are let loose to sift for treasure in rubble in the five-acre quarry.

Not to worry—there are no dangerous shafts or abrupt cliffs here. At its lowest point, the quarry is six feet deep. Yet those six feet hold evidence of life from 410 million years ago, when Chicago was covered by a tropical sea. If your kids find fossils, the naturalist will help them identify their discoveries.

This program, like almost every program at Camp Sagawau and other Forest Preserve District nature centers, is free. It's offered three times a year in spring, summer, and fall. (Call early to make your reservation.) Wear sturdy shoes and expect to spend a couple of fascinating hours with your pint-size paleontologists!

Camp Sagawau
12545 W. 111th Street
Lemont
(708) 257-2045
Preregistration is necessary for all programs except canyon hikes.

Big Town on the Prairie

In a handful of spots within the Forest Preserve District, you and your children can get a taste of the landscape that first greeted settlers to the Prairie State: thousands of acres of prairie grasses so tall that a person on horseback couldn't see over it.

To help the District restore its land to presettlement conditions, volunteers devote countless hours to nurturing Cook County prairies and oak savannas (a habitat even rarer than tallgrass prairie) back to health.

Some of these prairies and savannas are in nature preserves you can visit any time. But it's more illuminating to visit in the company of an expert who can reveal the prairie's secrets, like the long, hidden roots that help plants ride out droughts, and the curious way a devastating fire stimulates growth of the plants' lush blossoms.

A guide can tell your family what the land was like in presettlement times and explain how agriculture and urban development changed the prairie and squeezed out some species. A guide can also explain the restoration process and show kids how each activity—seed collecting, controlled burning, removing unwanted species—nudges the prairie back to life.

Organized tours of prairies under restoration are few and far between, because the first priority of the volunteers is to reclaim the prairie. Occasionally a work group will host an open house or set up a tour through the Nature Conservancy. To find out when and where these events are held, call Camp Sagawau ([708] 257-2045). Its volunteer coordinator can give you the phone number of the stewards in charge of restoration projects in the Poplar Creek, North Branch, Salt Creek, Des Plaines, Palos, and Calumet Divisions. The volunteer stewards will be glad to tell you how to find the prairie and when to visit.

If your kids are over 12, they might enjoy lending a hand on a prairie work day. The best task for kids is seed stripping, which means a fall work day may be most appropriate. Call first to find out when a work day is scheduled and your family can drop by to lend a hand or watch the restoration process at one of these sites:

- Cap Sauers Holdings in Sag Valley Division, Route 83 one mile west of Willow Spring Road

- Oxbow Prairie in Bunker Hill Forest Preserve; on the west side of Caldwell Avenue a quarter mile north of Devon Avenue

- Sauganash Prairie, on the south side of Bryn Mawr Avenue, east of Cicero Avenue

- Shoe Factory Road Nature Preserve in the Poplar Creek Forest Preserve on the west side of Route 59, north of Golf Road

The easiest way to visit a prairie is to watch the schedules at nature centers that have substantial prairie holdings. Camp Sagawau, Sand Ridge Nature Center, and Crabtree Nature Center all hold regular prairie walks hosted by naturalists who can clue your family in to this uniquely midwestern habitat.

A Day in the Country at the Palos and Sag Valley Preserves

If you're looking for a quick escape from the city, try visiting the Palos and Sag Valley Preserves. The largest contiguous forest preserve in Cook County, this preserve offers 10,000 acres of rolling hills, verdant forests, and lapping sloughs–all just forty-five minutes south of downtown Chicago. It's the fastest and cheapest way to spend a day in the country with your family.

Armed with trail maps from the Forest Preserve District, you can plan a ramble by a slough, through a woods, or along the Illinois & Michigan Canal. You can bring your bikes, walk, or just spread out a blanket and soak up a little peace and quiet.

If you're visiting on a weekend when Camp Sagawau is offering a canyon hike, don't miss it. When you're tired of walking, take your family to the Little Red Schoolhouse and cluck over its cute animal residents, or sit along the levee of the Chicago Sanitary and Ship Canal and watch the barges go by.

To really tire your kid out, make a warm-weather pilgrimage to the Swallow Cliff toboggan chutes on Route 83 west of Mannheim Road. You and your kids can run up and down the stairs that lead to the top of the chutes–and at the top, you'll be rewarded by a wonderful view of the surrounding forest preserves!

More Great Outdoors

An enormous public lakefront . . . stands of century-old trees . . . a river that made Chicago a major trade center . . . these and other wonders give your kids space to run, jump, shout, and learn about the region around us.

Outdoor Opportunities

A wonderful way to learn about natural history hikes, workshops, and outings is by reading *Prairie University*. Published twice a year by the Illinois Field Office of the Nature Conservancy, this is a guide to educational and volunteer opportunities in natural history and ecological restoration in northeastern Illinois. Although people who want to participate in various land stewardship and restoration projects are its primary audience, it contains information about family activities, classes, and tours sponsored by nature centers and organizations throughout our area.

You can pick up a free copy from the Nature Conservancy, or order one by sending a check for $2 to cover postage and handling. Mark your envelope "Attention Prairie University."

The Nature Conservancy
79 W. Monroe Street
Chicago, IL 60603
346-8166

Lincoln Park

Weeping willows, formal gardens, a farm, a zoo, and expanses of green lawn that invite somersaults and races—these delights and more await your family on an afternoon in Lincoln Park.

You'll find the greatest number of activities between Armitage and Diversey Avenues: the Lincoln Park Zoo and Farm-in-the-Zoo, the Lincoln Park Conservatory, paddle boats, horse and carriage rides, the Lincoln Park Boat Club, a miniature golf range, and an array of concessions offering ice cream, soda, and other kid snacks.

Wide, stroller-friendly paths wend their way through this part of the park. If you're feeling particularly ambitious, you can rent a paddle boat and explore the South Pond. Parents, be sure to join your kids; paddling is hard work and little kids will need your help. The big paddle boats fit five people, the small ones three. Kids must be tall enough to reach the peddles and need to wear the life preservers provided by the concession. The operator of this concession may change from season to season; for the current phone number, call the Park District's main information line: 747-2200.

North of the zoo, you can stop for ice cream at Cafe Brauer, or saunter through the gardens on your way to the Lincoln Park Conservatory. East of the zoo, you can sit at the water's edge and watch people rowing and paddling the length of the Lincoln Park Lagoon. (To join them, visit the Lincoln Park Boat Club, described in chapter 7, "Maritime Chicago.") Cross the pedestrian bridge and you'll be at the lake, where you can unroll your towel and unpack your picnic basket at North Avenue Beach, one of the city's best lakeside spots.

There are bathrooms aplenty in this part of the park. Look for them in the Farm-in-the-Zoo, Lincoln Park Zoo, and Cafe Brauer.

Your afternoon in the park can even include a miniature golf game, if you walk as far as Diversey Avenue. Next to the Diversey Driving Range at Diversey Avenue and Sheridan Road, is an eighteen-hole course open spring, summer, and fall from 7:00 A.M. to 9:00 P.M. A game costs a reasonable $3 for kids and $4 for adults. Call 281-5722 for more information.

A Horse and Carriage Ride through the Park

Tired of walking? Try traveling Lincoln Park's charming paths via horse and carriage.

During warm-weather weekends, Antique Coach and Carriage offers twenty-five-minute rides through the park. Less expensive and more relaxed than carriage rides through Near North traffic, a park carriage ride is ideal for families. Up to six people can ride for a mere $20, and the trip is short enough that kids won't get bored.

Carriage rides are offered on Saturday and Sunday from 10:00 A.M. to 5:00 P.M., whenever the weather is nice. The horses stay home when it's raining or extremely hot. If you want to treat your family to a carriage ride, call Antique Coach first to confirm that the carriages are operating.

Antique Coach and Carriage
787-1349

A City Forest

A forest near Lincoln Park? Yes—on Arlington Place, just east of Clark Street. (Arlington is one block north of Fullerton Avenue, and runs east toward Lincoln Park.) Once a 75-by-100-foot empty lot, the forest was nurtured by a resident who began planting trees in the early seventies. Now operated as a bird sanctuary by the Chicago Audubon Society, it is home to raccoons, squirrels, and other small animals. For safety reasons, the lot is fenced off, but there's plenty to see from the sidewalk.

In the winter, kids can see animal tracks in the snow. In the spring, trees and bushes burst into flower. In summer, it's a deep, shady glade; and in the fall, it's a riot of color, a miniature fall foliage trip without the hassle of the long drive. In any season, it's a refreshing peek at wilderness for young city dwellers.

North Park Village Nature Center

In a little piece of wilderness at the corner of Peterson and Kedzie Avenues, your kids can enjoy a Sunday afternoon stroll, an evening star watch, or a middle-of-the-night owl prowl. The sixty-one-acre North Park Village Nature Center is so small that the roar of traffic never dies, but this patch of country in the city offers an abundance of outdoor family programs.

Once a tree nursery and later a tuberculosis sanitarium, the center is being restored to its presettler condition by naturalists and volunteers who can lead you on a fascinating trip down its trails. You'll stroll by a pond full of rushes, see stewards tending fires or planting seeds, and learn the secrets of stems, leaves, and grasses. Make sure you bring along binoculars and magnifying glasses, so your kids can watch for birds and examine bugs and tree bark.

Inside the center, your family can visit resident turtles, rabbits, and animals injured in the wild, or learn more about the northeastern Illinois habitat from informative displays on geology, botany, and other natural history topics. Bring a state identification card or a library card with you, and your family will be issued a card that entitles you to borrow from the collection of several hundred nature books—many for kids—in its lending library. Even without lending privileges, you can borrow a field guide to take along on your hike through the center grounds.

Owned by the City of Chicago and funded by the Department of Environment, North Park Village is a hive of activities for kids of all ages. Preschoolers can take monthlong nature activity classes (these very popular classes fill quickly); older kids can enjoy hands-on workshops like the owl discovery hour, when kids inspect owl pellets and reconstruct a typical owl dinner, see a video on owls, and meet a live great horned owl. After school, kids can attend nature story hours and hear exciting tales, like *The Sign of the Beaver*, the story of a boy learning to survive in the wild with the aid of Native Americans.

At night, the center sponsors star watches, family campfires, and middle-of-the-night owl prowls. Seasonal change is celebrated by imaginative special events like the March Maple Syrup Festival, when your family can see how maple sap is tapped, and watch as it is boiled down into sweet syrup you can taste right off the fire.

Even in winter, the nature center is bustling with special programs. In fact, a snowy January Sunday is one of the best times to visit. When everything is still and blanketed in fresh snow, your kids can see tracks and other signs left behind by animals and learn how these animals adapt to and survive the harsh weather.

In June, the nature center sponsors EcoExplorers, weeklong nature summer camps that end with a family bonfire and sing-along.

The best way to tap into this wealth of nature programs is to get on the nature center's mailing list. Ask to receive the *Urban Naturalist*, the center's seasonal calendar of events, and you'll be first in line to register for dozens of family adventures.

North Park Village Nature Center
5801 N. Pulaski Road
744-5472

The Inland Waterway: The Chicago River

Far from a victim of industrial pollution, the Chicago River is teeming with life. Deer, red foxes, snapping turtles, blue and green heron, and numerous species of birds and fishes live along its shores. Even at the North Avenue turning basin, one of the most polluted spots on the river, fish and beavers flourish.

People thrive along the Chicago River, too. For proof, visit the charming Ravenswood Manor neighborhood and take a walk across the Wilson Avenue bridge. From the bridge you'll see homes whose gardens spill down to the water's edge, small docks where private boats are moored, and tall trees that make the city seem a million miles away.

The river is also brimming with stories about Chicago's economic, political, and cultural history. The best way to discover its secrets is to ramble along the river's edge with the Friends of the Chicago River.

All FOCR tours focus on the Chicago River's role in the development of the city and current issues that affect the river's viability. Walks along the river in the forest preserves focus on wildlife and habitat, while walks in the city examine the river's role in the city's cultural history and explain how it influenced the neighborhoods along its banks.

For kids, the primo FOCR tour is the visit to Bubbly Creek (near the corner of Ashland and Archer Avenues), where the river bubbles eerily beneath your feet. Its bubbles are a legacy of its years as a repository for animal carcasses tossed out by the nearby stockyards. Legend has it that at one time it was so choked with carcasses, a person could walk across it. The carcasses eventually attracted soap manufacturers, who found Bubbly Creek a great source of raw material. They skimmed the fat off the surface and took it back to their factories for processing.

Today's bubbles are created partly by a century of waste and partly by present-day overflow from a nearby pumping station. The knowledgeable FOCR docents can tell your kids all sorts of gross details they'll just love.

Another tour with kid appeal is the Elbow Tour, which meets at the Eighteenth Street bridge. During this tour, which follows the river's south branch before it bends to meet Bubbly Creek, you visit five different movable bridges and learn how each one works. On a couple of occasions, the tour group has been invited into a bridge tender's house for a closer look at its operation. (You could combine this tour with a visit to the Skybox for Rail Fans, 329 W. Eighteenth Street. See chapter 8, "Trains and Planes.")

Try the Goose Island or the LaBagh Woods tours on the river's north branch. The Goose Island tour offers interesting insights into the North Avenue turning basin, and lets you visit Chicago's only island, where warehouses and factories take advantage of easy transportation provided by the river. On the LaBagh Woods tour your family strolls through a lovely forest while you hear about the river's roots as a natural prairie stream.

The Main Branch and the Mouth of the River tours let kids see a familiar territory in new light. On the Main Branch tour you will walk along the Loop, looking at the river instead of the buildings. The Mouth of the River tour explores the engineering feats that reversed the river, and the locks that divide the lake from the river. (Sadly, there is no way to visit the locks themselves, short of buying a ticket on the Wendella Sightseeing Boats.)

Chicago River tours are held rain or shine every Saturday and Sunday from May through October. Walking tours last about two and a half hours and cover two and a half miles. They are best for kids 8 and older who can go two hours without a bathroom pit stop. Wear sturdy shoes, and if it's hot, wear hats and sunglasses and bring water. There is no need to make reservations; simply show up at the meeting place and pay $5 per person. You can also purchase a map of the river that will inspire river trips on your own.

If you're more ambitious, try an FOCR canoe trip. These all-day adventures feature a little talk and a lot of paddling, although the pace is relaxed. And children are welcome! The canoe routes are:

- a loop around the Skokie Lagoons (including a fall color tour)

- the Forgotten River Tour—from just north of Devon and Caldwell Avenues to just south of Foster Avenue (includes a lunch break and a walk on the prairie)

- a very scenic tour through the forest preserves of the far north branch, from Willow Road to Devon Avenue

- the Loop the Goose Tour, beginning at the mouth of the river, goes north around Goose Island and back to the river's mouth

(Looking up at Loop skyscrapers from a canoe is an experience not to be missed!)

Kids who have some experience in a canoe or who are 10 or older may help paddle with a partner. Younger children can come along for the ride and sit safely in the middle of the canoe—*if* they are mature enough to spend a day there. Be aware that these trips last all day and that there are no bathrooms, although in a pinch a wooded shore may do!

Good news for families who want to see the river without paddling themselves: as this book went to press, Friends of the Chicago River was preparing to launch a boat tour. Plans call to have the boat sail south to Eighteenth Street, north to Goose Island, and out onto the lake, with an FOCR docent on board to discuss history, ecology, water quality, and points of interest, and to fascinate your family with little-known river lore.

An annual schedule of walking tours and canoe and boat trips conducted by Friends of the Chicago River is ready in late March. Call to get a copy, and add our overlooked inland waterway to your family itinerary!

Friends of the Chicago River
407 S. Dearborn Street, Suite 1580
939-0490

Chicago Botanic Garden

Twenty-five miles north of Chicago on Forest Preserve District land is the Chicago Botanic Garden, a 300-acre living museum where your family can savor the sights and smells of twenty different gardens and enjoy imaginative weekend activities for children and parents.

To decide which garden to visit first, stop by the Gateway Center to see *A Garden for All Seasons*, the six-minute video overview of the garden's programs and research activities. Another way to get the big picture without wearing out the kids is to ride the tram. This forty-five-minute narrated tour takes you through the entire garden, so you can see everything and then backtrack to the gardens you want to visit.

Fortunately, the paths are stroller friendly, and almost all of the gardens are conveniently located on the garden's main island. If you're in the mood for a longer walk, stroll around the lagoons of the Skokie River and visit the fifteen-acre prairie, which features six different types of prairie habitats. Kids can take a bathroom break at the Children's Fruit and Vegetable Garden, about halfway around the trail.

Of the twenty gardens, five are true kid favorites. In the Waterfall Garden, entrancing, water-loving plants thrive at the base of a waterfall that cascades down forty-five feet from the Dwarf Conifer Garden. The path through the Waterfall Garden crosses lagoons and leads to the quiet, secluded Japanese Garden, a favorite among older children.

In the Sensory Garden, designed for people with visual impairments, there are plants to touch, smell, and listen to. Kids can feel leaves of different textures, or stand still and listen to the quiet rustling of leaves and branches. Kids also like the Fruit and Vegetable Garden and the English Walled Garden, reminiscent of the Secret Garden of book, movie, and musical fame.

For a walk in the woods, take the short, twisting path through the Turnbull Woods, fifteen acres of oak savanna being restored to its natural condition. In the spring there are plenty of wildflowers; in the fall, an abundance of color.

A visit to the Botanic Garden is rewarding even in cold winter months. The garden's greenhouses, a warm, colorful respite from frigid weather, are the center for many of the garden's weekend family activities. In January, you feel like you've escaped to the desert by working on projects and listening to stories related to the Desert Greenhouse. (For more about the Botanic Garden greenhouses, see chapter 9, "The Urban Jungle.")

Seasonal stories and hands-on projects are scheduled every Saturday and Sunday and are free with admission to the garden. During the Saturday story hours, which begin at 1:30 P.M., stories are told about seasons and habitats like deserts, jungles, and prairies. Drop-in workshops revolve around a different theme or garden. In the fall, kids can make leaf prints and pinecone bird feeders; in the spring, they can learn about worm farming and peek underground to see bulbs growing. Drop by these workshops any weekend between 1:00 and 4:00 P.M.

The Botanic Garden also offers midweek and weekend preschool story time, and a nifty overnight three or four times each summer. Call the Education Registrar for information regarding story times, and see chapter 13, "Sleep with the Fishes," for information about the kids only overnight.

The Botanic Garden is open every day except Christmas from 8:00 A.M. to sunset. Admission to the garden is free; parking costs $4. Wheelchair-accessible parking is available in parking lots 1, 2, and 3. Wheelchairs are available on a first-come, first-served basis from the information desk in the Gateway Center. A driver's license or the equivalent will be held at the information desk until the wheelchair is returned.

The forty-five-minute guided, narrated tour of the entire garden costs $3.50 for adults, $1.75 for kids and seniors.

The Food for Thought Cafe in the Gateway Center is open for breakfast and lunch. Picnics may be eaten in a picnic area located between parking lots 1 and 2.

Roller blading and bicycling are not allowed inside the Botanic Garden, though strollers are welcome.

Chicago Botanic Garden
1000 Lake Cook Road, east of Edens Expressway
Glencoe
General information: (708) 835-5440
Education registrar: (708) 835-8261

The Chicago Botanic Garden

The Chicago Botanic Garden is a place full of flowers and a wonderful place to relax. It is also full of information about plants and how different people use many kinds of plants for medicine, food, clothing, and even shelter.

Outside they have a nature trail overlooking a beautiful lake, surrounded by hundreds of magnificent geese.

—Abigail Rundquist
West Rogers Park

Simple Things Your Kids Can Do to Save the Planet

For most boomer parents, the Scout leader's exhortation to "leave the campsite cleaner than you found it" was about the closest they came to an environmental education.

Today's kids are considerably more sophisticated about the state of the world around them. It's no surprise that they love nature, and often want to lend it a hand. All of the organizations listed here sponsor special cleanup and restoration activities where your child's labor and enthusiasm will be welcomed.

Count Butterflies. Each July, the North Park Village Nature Center and the Illinois Audubon Society cosponsor the Xerxes Society Annual North American Butterfly Count. Adults and children are welcome to take a census of a dozen local species and learn more about monarchs, tiger swallowtails, and other butterfly species. Sign up by calling North Park Village Nature Center at 744-5472.

Clean a Park, Playlot, or Beach. Before you take your sand shovels and buckets to the beach, why not grab a full-size rake and help clean then? Friends of the Parks offers three clean up events for families: the Earth Day Parks Cleanup in April, the Playlot Cleanup in May, and the Great Lakes Beach Sweep in September. Call Friends of the Park at 922-3307 for dates and details.

Rescue the River. Your kids can make their mark on the river by participating in the Great Chicago River Rescue Day, held in May. Take a Saturday and lend a hand at one of a dozen sites along the north and south branches. For details about this watershed-wide cleanup, call Friends of the Chicago River at 939-0490.

Kids clear debris from a riverbank during Chicago River Rescue Day. *Photo by Michael T. Konrath.*

Be a Mighty Acorn. Suggest that your child's school participates in the Mighty Acorns, a conservancy program for kids from third grade through middle school, and you can accompany the class on its workday.

Funded by the Forest Preserve District of Cook County and coordinated by the Nature Conservancy, the Mighty Acorns program takes kids to sites where they do restoration work under adult supervision (the adult-to-child ratio is 1:5). Docents visit the classroom before and after the field day, which begins with a walk and an orientation for the children to the habitat they will be working in.

After spending a day collecting seeds or cutting buckthorn, the kids return to the classroom for more environmental studies, and eventually return to the work site in another season. To find out about the Mighty Acorns, call the Nature Conservancy at 346-8166.

12

Winter Wonderland

When the weather outside is frightful, families have two choices: pretend it's warmer, or put on hats and gloves and plunge right into a snowbank!

This chapter can help you plan an old-fashioned winter afternoon of ice-skating, sledding, or cross-country skiing. But don't postpone your winter fun until it's too late! By March and April, Chicago's snowy winter wonderland gives way to gray, drab, boring weeks that are too late for fun in the snow—but a perfect time for a trip to one of the steamy greenhouses discussed in chapter 9, "The Urban Jungle."

When It's Cold, Party!

When the January wind is blowing, and there's snow on the ground, why not embrace the season at the Forest Preserve District of Cook County's Winter Festival?

To give everyone a chance to celebrate, the Forest Preserve District thoughtfully throws *two* parties on two different dates in January. Northsiders can party at Jensen Slides, 6400 W. Devon Avenue at Milwaukee Avenue in Chicago; southsiders can celebrate a week later at Swallow Cliff, Route 83 west of Mannheim Road in Palos Park.

Because everything except the refreshments is free, the Winter Festival is a cheap family date. All chute fees are waived, so you can toboggan to your heart's content using your own sleds and toboggans, or borrow the District's toboggans at no charge.

When the kids are tired of sliding, they can cross-country ski or watch the snow show and ice-sculpting demonstrations. The brawny employees of the Forestry Department demonstrate woodcutting skills and will let your kids pair off and use (under supervision) a two-person saw. If your family wants to learn more about the woods in winter, pick up a map and set off on a nature scavenger hunt that reveals winter's subtle wonders. When everyone is tired of physical activity, curl up together in a horse-drawn sleigh for a marvelous ride through the woods. (If there's no snow, there will be a hay ride instead.)

Winter Festival activities are centered around the toboggan chutes. Within a few hundred yards of the chutes, you'll find refreshments, demonstrations, craft activities, puppet shows, and gigantic roaming polar bears and penguins. There are warming shelters at both locations, and bathrooms at Jensen Slides. (Swallow Cliff has outhouses only.) The festivities start at 11:00 A.M. and last until 3:00 P.M. For more information, call the Special Events Office of the Forest Preserve District of Cook County at (708) 771-1014.

Ice-Skating

Most old-time Chicagoans can tell you about winters of yore, when the neighborhood school yard or park was transformed into a skating rink with a simple garden hose.

Alas, personal injury settlements have severely reduced opportunities for casual skating. But in the right weather conditions, the Park District still floods selected parks for ice-skating. With sixty-five skating rinks created each winter, chances are there's one near you. To get a list of outdoor rinks, call the Chicago Park District's Landscaping Department at 747-0792.

If you don't have your own skates, you'll have to plan your outing for a location that rents skates. Two that offer great skating plus dramatic views are Skate on State and the Daley Bicentennial Plaza.

The City of Chicago operates Skate on State (Washington and State Streets, 744-2889), a rink that's open from Thanksgiving through early March. Its dramatic setting in the heart of the Loop guarantees an unforgettable outing. Unfortunately, it also guarantees a big crowd, and the lines for skate rental can be very, very long.

If you can't bring your own skates, plan to visit early in the day. The rink opens at 9:00 A.M. and is relatively uncrowded on weekdays until 11:00 A.M., and between 2:30 and 5:00 P.M. If you visit on a Monday, Wednesday, or Friday morning, your family can stay and watch the noon demonstrations by local skaters. Free figure-skating lessons are offered on Saturday and hockey-skating lessons on Sunday from 9:00 to 11:00 A.M. Saturday is also a heavy skate day; Sunday is lighter. The rink closes at 7:15 P.M.

Skates cost $3 for adults and $2 for kids. You can check coats and bags in the skate rental trailer for just $1, and change and warm up in two other trailers. There are plenty of portable toilets, including some that are handicapped accessible.

For little or no waiting, skate at the Daley Bicentennial Plaza at 337 E. Randolph Street (742-7650). This Park District–operated facility boasts a spacious, groomed rink, a wide supply of rental skates, and a warming room where you can rest and have a cup of hot chocolate. (Parking is simple, too: only $5 for up to 24 hours at the nearby Monroe Street garage.)

During skating season, Daley Plaza is open Monday through Friday from 10:00 A.M. to 10:00 P.M., and Saturday and Sunday from 10:00 A.M. to 5:00 P.M. On weekdays, you can skate whenever you please, but to give everyone a turn on weekends and winter school vacation days, skating is scheduled in two-hour sessions (10:00 A.M. to 12:00, 12:30 to 2:30 P.M., 3:00 to 5:00 P.M.; additional sessions run during December holiday weekdays, from 5:30 to 7:30 P.M. and 8:00 to 10:00 P.M.). During the half-hour break, the Zamboni machine comes out to groom the ice—a treat for kids who like big machines.

Railings surround the rink, so fledgling skaters can hang on for dear life or keep one hand on the railing and the other in yours. Plans are afoot to offer skating lessons; call the Plaza for information about times and prices.

Weeknights are a wonderful time for a family skate. It's dark, cold, and crisp, and the towers of the Prudential Buildings and Randolph Street condominiums tower over you as you skate. When you tire, you can sit inside and enjoy a cup of hot chocolate from a vending machine until everyone is ready to hit the ice again.

An midweek evening skate can be an inexpensive and fun family date. Besides a $1 rink fee, parents pay $1.50 and kids under 14 only $1 to rent skates. You can stash your stuff in lockers that cost $.10, or you bring your own lock and pay nothing at all. The bathrooms are great, the lounge area is remarkably comfortable, and the rink won't be crowded at all.

If you do decide to skate on the weekend, be aware that the 10:00 A.M. session is the least crowded, and the 3:00 P.M. session is the most crowded. Friday evenings are busier than other weeknights, but you should not have any trouble getting skates.

To *really* feel like Hans Brinker, you can take your family skating on real ponds and lakes in the Forest Preserve. When the ice is at least four inches thick, skating is permitted at these sites:

- Barrington Road Pond, on Barrington Road south of Higgins Road in Hoffman Estates
- Buffalo Woods, Kean Avenue north of Eighty-seventh Street in Willow Springs
- Busse Woods (north pool), Higgins Road west of Arlington Heights Road in Elk Grove Village
- Cermak Quarry, 7600 West Ogden Avenue in Lyons
- Crawdad Slough, 104th Avenue south of 95th Street in Willow Springs
- Deer Grove, Quentin Road north of Dundee Road in Palatine
- Hambone Lake, 135th Street and Harlem Avenue in Palos Heights

- Hidden Pond East, Kean Avenue north of Ninety-fifth Street in Hickory Hills

- Papoose Lake, 123rd Street west of LaGrange Road in Palos Hills

- Powderhorn Lake, east of Burnham Avenue and north of Brainard Avenue in Calumet City

- Schiller Woods, Irving Park Road and Cumberland Avenue in Schiller Park

- Wampum Lake, Thornton-Lansing Road, east of Thornton Road in Thornton

Call (708) 366-9420 before you go to find out which ponds have reached the magic four-inch mark!

Finally, year-round ice-skating and great ice-skating lessons are available at **McFetridge Sports Complex** (3845 N. California Avenue, 742-7585). Open skating sessions are held Wednesday and Friday afternoons from 3:30 to 5:00 P.M., and Saturday and Sunday from 4:30 to 6:00 P.M. Skates can be rented for $2 a pair; the rink fee is $2.50 for adults, $2 for high-school students, and $1.50 for kids under 13.

Sledding and Coasting Hills

The Forest Preserve District of Cook County permits sledding and coasting at these locations when there are four inches of snow on the ground and the temperature is below twenty degrees:

- Dan Ryan Woods North, Eighty-seventh Street and Western Avenue (no shelter, outhouses only)

- Deer Grove, Quentin Road north of Dundee Road in Palatine (no shelter, outhouses only)

- Indian Hills Woods, Sixteenth Street and Edgewood Avenue in Chicago Heights (no amenities)

- Jensen Sports Area, Devon and Milwaukee Avenues (shelters and bathrooms)

- Pioneer Woods, 107th Street, a half mile west of LaGrange Road (no shelter, outhouses only)

- Schiller Woods, Irving Park Road and Cumberland Avenue (no shelter, outhouses only)

- Westchester Woods, Cermak Road east of LaGrange Road (no shelter, bathroom, or outhouse!)

Call the Forest Preserve District at (708) 366-9420 to check conditions and availability. These sledding areas are open from 8:00 A.M. until sunset.

Tobogganing

Is sledding too wimpy for your pint-size thrill seeker? Then spend a day at one of the toboggan slides operated by the Forest Preserve District of Cook County.

It's a long climb to the top, but once there kids can enjoy a stomach-churning hurtle down a chute that ranges from 170 to 376 feet long at one of these slides:

- Bemis Woods, Ogden Avenue west of Wolf Road in Western Springs, plunges thirty-seven feet over a 170-foot-long course. Outhouses only; no bathrooms or warming shelter. Call (708) 246-8366.

- Dan Ryan Woods, Eighty-seventh Street and Western Avenue in Chicago, has a 200-foot-long course with a forty-five-foot vertical drop. There is a warming shelter with bathrooms. Call 233-3766.

- Deer Grove 5, Quentin Road north of Dundee Road in Palatine, drops fifty-five feet over a 270-foot-long course. No bathrooms; outhouses and warming shelter only. Call (708) 381-7868.

- Jensen Slides, Devon and Milwaukee Avenues in Chicago, has a 240-foot-long course with a thirty-four-foot drop. There are bathrooms and a warming shelter. Call 631-7657.

• Swallow Cliff, Route 83 west of Mannheim Road in Palos Park. The granddaddy of all slides has six chutes that plunge a heart-stopping ninety feet over a 376-foot-long course! There are outhouses and a warming shelter. Call (708) 448-4417.

Whenever there are proper conditions (four inches of snow on the ground and the temperature is under twenty degrees), these slides are open daily from 10:00 A.M. to 10:00 P.M. Your family may bring its own toboggan, but it will be inspected first to make sure it fits in the chutes, is not damaged, and has no potentially dangerous splinters. If you bring your own, you'll pay a $1 chute pass fee that is good all day. If you rent toboggans from the Forest Preserve District, the chute pass fee is included in the price of the toboggan.

For $3 an hour, you can rent a six-foot toboggan that fits three, a seven-footer for four, or an eight-footer for six people. You'll have to surrender your driver's license or leave a $40 cash deposit when you check out your vehicle.

Toboggan rides are fast and thrilling—perhaps too thrilling for very young children. That's why kids should be at least thirty-six inches tall before they venture onto the toboggan chutes. For safety's sake and to comply with the rules, young children should always be accompanied by parents on any of these toboggan chutes. Hold on tight!

Cross-Country Skiing in the Forest Preserve

You don't have to drive to northern Wisconsin to enjoy cross-country skiing. There are hundreds of miles of ski trails in the Forest Preserve District—and a Nordic Ski School where you and your family can rent equipment and learn beginning and advanced cross-country skiing, ski skating, and Nordic downhill skiing.

From mid-December until the beginning of March, Camp Sagawau in the Palos Hills Forest Preserve is open daily for skiing. Its three and a half miles of trails, the only groomed trails in the

At Camp Sagawau's red farmhouse, your family can rent cross-country skis, sign up for ski lessons, or warm up by the woodstove in the living room. *Photo by Michael T. Konrath.*

Forest Preserve, open at 9:00 A.M. and close at sunset. An easy loop around Camp Sagawau's prairie and forest is accompanied by a more challenging trail along its ridge, which is one of the highest spots in Cook County (640 feet above sea level).

Start your ski day by checking in at Camp Sagawau's red farmhouse for a free trail pass, which you must display while skiing. Nearby are warming facilities, washrooms, and a drinking fountain—usually. Recent water quality problems have been known to shut down Camp Sagawau's water supplies and reduce facilities to a set of chemical toilets. Call first to make sure the water is working.

If you don't own ski equipment, you can rent it for $10 per person a day. You can rent traditional cross-country ski equipment for children and adults, or zippy, short ski skates. A driver's license or $40 cash deposit is required and parents must complete and sign rental consent forms for children under 18. The last equipment is rented at 3:00 P.M. No one under 18 can rent equipment, and all children under 12 must be supervised at all times.

On Saturdays in January and February, Camp Sagawau offers beginning and intermediate/advanced lessons. Lessons for beginners 12 and over begin at 9:30 A.M.; intermediate/advanced sessions start at 1:30 P.M. Lessons cost $10 a session; if you also rent equipment, the combined rental-lesson fee is $18.

You and your teenagers can enjoy a quiet, contemplative ski tour through Camp Sagawau's many habitats during the weekly Sunday afternoon Nature Ski Tour, when a Camp Sagawau naturalist points out secrets of the winter landscape. These slow-paced, two-hour tours begin Sundays at 1:30 P.M. No preregistration is required, beginners are welcome, and the tour is free.

Two weekends a season, the camp teaches basic skiing skills to kids 8 to 11, replacing the usual formal ski lesson with entertaining games and activities that help kids master the trick of standing up and sliding on skis.

Your family can ski at Camp Sagawau without making any special arrangements, but you need to preregister for lessons and kids' workshops. (No reservations are available for rentals.) You can call in your reservation on the Monday morning prior to the activity for which you are registering.

Whenever there's snow on the ground, Camp Sagawau is open—unless there has been an ice storm, or the thermometer drops below negative ten degrees. Call (708) 257-2045 for information about skiing conditions, lessons, rentals, or to request a brochure about the Camp Sagawau Nordic Ski Program.

In addition to Camp Sagawau, cross-country skiing is permitted on all trails and open areas of the Forest Preserve District, except for special use areas such as nature centers and golf courses. All trails are open from sunrise to sunset. Maps of the following seven major trail areas are available from Forest Preserve Headquarters:

● Arie Crown Forest, north of the Stevenson Expressway at Mannheim Road. Park in the Sundown Meadow parking lot on the west side of Mannheim Road north of Sixty-seventh Street. 3.45 miles of wooded trail with gentle slopes and flat terrain.

- Bemis Woods, on the north side of Ogden Avenue west of Wolf Road in Western Springs, near the toboggan slide. 4.5 miles of trail cover gently rolling terrain and are suitable for beginners.

- Beverly Lake Area, on Higgins Road one mile west of Sutton Road (Illinois Route 59). 2.3 hilly miles, suitable for intermediate skiers, pass through mature oak forests and open savannas.

- Camp Sagawau Area. See above for information.

- Deer Grove Preserve, west side of Quentin Road just north of Dundee Road in Palatine. Trail passes through mature oak and maple forests and over hilly terrain. Wooded areas provide protection from severe winds on cold days. 8.5 miles of trails.

- Maple Lake Area in Willow Springs. Enter on Archer Avenue north of Route 83. Hilly terrain and mature forests make this trail especially suited to the intermediate and expert skier. An expert section is north of Bullfrog Lake. About 7 miles of trails.

- Swallow Cliff Area. Start at Swallow Cliff toboggan slides on Route 83 (111th Street) and U.S. Interstate 45. 6.2 miles of rolling terrain. Warming center and heated rest rooms are available at toboggan slides.

••

The Forest Preserve District of Cook County publishes a brochure listing all of its winter sports facilities, which also includes listings for snowmobiling and ice fishing. A set of seven maps provides details about the designated cross-country trails and the Camp Sagawau ski area. To get copies, call (708) 366-9420. You can also call this number to find out whether the sledding hills and ice rinks are open and ready for your visit!

••

The Forest After Dark

Want to ski under the stars and enjoy the beauty of the forest after dark? Take your family on the Moonlight Ski at Deer Grove.

As you ski through the forest, candles light your way and illuminate the bare trees around you. At four stations in the forest, there are glowing bonfires where you can take a break and warm up. Mom and Dad can enjoy wine and cheese at these stations; kids are served a cup of piping hot chocolate. When you finish the trail loop, your family can relax in the warming house or go outside and play in the snow without skis.

The Moonlight Ski is held once a year in February at the Deer Grove Woods in Palatine (on Quentin Road north of Dundee Road). If there's little or no snow, the event becomes a moonlight hike. For more information about the ski, call the Forest Preserve District's Special Events Office at (708) 771-1014.

13

Sleep with the Fishes

Great Family Overnights

If you were a heavy reader as a child, you may remember E. L. Konigsburg's *From the Mixed Up Files of Mrs. Basil E. Frankweiler*, in which two children run away from home and take up residence in the Metropolitan Museum of Art.

Back then, all we could do was dream about it—but today, you and your family *can* spend the night in a museum. Or a zoo. Or an aquarium. Or a planetarium! Just about every major Chicago institution offers special overnight adventures that are cheaper than a week in Disney World, and just as exciting. All of them offer unique accommodations, great activities, and a chance to explore in peace and at length institutions that are often packed during daylight hours.

A few general ground rules apply to all of these overnight events.

Expect to stay up very, very late. No one settles down to sleep before 11:00 P.M. At the Field Museum, the lights are on until 2:00 A.M.! Count on someone in your family to fall apart, throw a tantrum, or otherwise display the stress of staying up late. If your children aren't night owls or need lots of sleep to be civil, hold off on your overnight until they are older.

Expect to get up very, very early. To prepare for daytime crowds, these institutions need to clear the halls early. At the Museum of Science and Industry, the coal mine whistle blows at 6:30 A.M. to rouse visitors for breakfast. Expect to be awakened between 6:00 and 7:00 A.M.

Bring a flashlight. On a flashlight tour, even familiar sights take on a decidedly mysterious air. Don't miss the fun by leaving yours at home!

Bring an air mattress. You'll only be sleeping for a few hours anyway, so why toss and turn? An air mattress or some kind of pad to place under a sleeping bag will help grown-ups sleep more comfortably and feel less irritable in the morning.

Remember where you put your stuff. When you sleep in an institution that lets you choose where to sleep, make sure everyone in the family knows the location of your camp. When it's 1:00 A.M., you'll want to turn in, not turn out a search party to find your sleeping bags.

Leave very small children at home. Family overnights aren't going to go away, so don't hurry a small child into a stressful evening in an unfamiliar place. These events appeal most to kids who are elementary-school age and up. Depending on the institution, even teenagers will be excited. Most institutions have a minimum age limit.

Don't worry about emergencies. These events are carefully planned. At the Museum of Science and Industry and the Field Museum, security guards keep an eye on vehicles and will be happy to escort you to your car if you forget something. The Field Museum keeps an emergency medical technician on hand to handle unexpected illnesses or injuries. To ensure your comfort and safety, your hosts will hardly sleep at all. They'll go to great lengths to make sure your evening is a happy and rewarding one.

Reserve early. Some institutions limit overnights to as few as 40 guests, others admit 800. But these are popular events and the list fills quickly!

Here's a rundown of the overnight adventures offered by major Chicago institutions.

Adler Planetarium

Like Wynken, Blynken, and Nod, your family can sleep in a sea of stars—*if* you are members of the Adler Planetarium!

The members-only Adler Planetarium overnight is limited to 100 people, including families with children ages 6 through 12. Kids are divided into two groups (ages 6–8 and 9–12) for structured activities related to astronomy. Crafts, building tours, and a sky show are also part of the evening. Very occasionally, overnight guests are invited up to the dome observatory to view the night sky over Chicago. Families sleep in the galleries, and the lights go out at midnight.

The overnight costs $30 per person. For information on membership, call 322-0332.

Brookfield Zoo

The Brookfield Zoo's Wild Night Overnight is an educational, all-night romp that gives a select group of families a chance to see how Brookfield denizens behave after dark. With only fifty guests admitted each time, your family will be almost alone with the animals inside the zoo's 215-acre park!

Wild Night starts at 6:00 P.M. with behind-the-scenes tours of various animal houses. You'll have a chance to ask the keepers everything you ever wanted to know about their duties and their animal charges. After the animal house visits, you can dust off your little-used nighttime senses on the ninety-minute night hike. Families use flashlights to pay a call to the big cat grottos, and then circle the lake at the zoo's forested west end. Don't be surprised if the wolves who live there greet you with a chorus of howls. (Relax. They're in cages.)

After the night hike, you'll be treated to a lavish snack and presented with a wide choice of activities in the Discovery Center whose carpeted classroom floors are your home for the night. There are movies about nocturnal animals, simple craft projects, and zoo games that teach lessons about habitat conservation. In one game about eco-tourism, kids act as rulers of small island nations as they evaluate various tourism scenarios that affect native animal populations.

In the morning after breakfast (served at 6:00 A.M.), your family can enjoy a bird-watching walk or visiting kangaroos and other animals that are most active in the morning (and hardly rouse themselves the rest of the day!). For kids who want to pretend this is a Saturday morning like any other, there are cartoons on the big screen. Wild Night wraps up with a tour of another animal house and a meeting with its keeper. Everyone goes home at 9:30 A.M.

Wild Night Overnight is offered about five times a year during spring and fall months. Members pay $35; nonmembers pay $45. The minimum age is 8. For more information about how to register for a Wild Night Overnight, call the Brookfield Zoo's Education Department at (708) 485-0263, ext. 361.

Chicago Botanic Garden

Extra, extra! Read all about it! Only kids are allowed at Chicago Botanic Garden summer overnights!

Sorry, parents. Kids 9 and 10 years old are the only ones who get to enjoy adventures like Nature at Night, a Japanese Adventure, and the popular Whodunnit? murder mystery.

The overnight includes unique activities related to the evening's theme. During Whodunnit?, roles in the mystery are played by adults, who leave it up to kids to conduct forensic science experiments to discover the culprit. During Nature at Night, there are games and talks on nocturnal creatures, and a spooky evening hike through the woods.

Besides crafts and projects, kids get to enjoy bedtime snacks, breakfast, and the chance to sleep in the Fruit and Vegetable Auditorium or the Educational Center.

Offered three times a summer, Chicago Botanic Garden overnights begin at 7:00 P.M. and end at 9:00 A.M. the next morning. All 9- and 10-year-olds are welcome. Call the Education Registrar at (708) 835-8261 for information about dates, themes, and prices of overnight events and other exciting kid programs.

Field Museum

Ever seen a dinosaur by flashlight? You can when you spend the night in the Field Museum! But don't expect to turn in early or sleep late. Your family will want to stay up as long as it can to enjoy the unique treat of having the halls of the Field to itself.

During the evening, your family will enjoy special tours and workshops that focus on topics like dinosaurs, or African and Native American cultures. The forty-five-minute workshops feature lectures and take-home crafts that relate to various Field exhibits. You can go on guided tours of the exhibits, a self-guided flashlight tour, or listen to a storytelling performance.

After a late-night snack, your family can roam the museum alone, pick up a map for a scavenger hunt through the collections, or attend additional workshops. Lights go off in the sleeping area–the carpeted Native American Halls–at 11:00 P.M., but night owls can explore the museum until 2:00 A.M., when the remaining lights finally go off. (The second floor is off-limits after 1:00 A.M.)

Breakfast is served from 7:30 to 8:00 A.M. in the Picnic in the Field area, and families leave before the museum opens at 9:00 A.M.

Overnights are offered monthly (except December) to families with children in first through sixth grades. About 300 people attend each time. The cost of the overnight is $35 for members, $40 for nonmembers. Contact the Education Department at 322-8854 to reserve your family's spot.

Lincoln Park Zoo

What do zoo animals do when the lights go out at the zoo? Find out at the Ark After Dark Zoo Overnighter, when your kids can see zoo animals at night and learn their nocturnal secrets from the nighttime zookeepers.

This event begins at 8:00 P.M. with a flashlight journey through the Kovler Lion House, the Fisher Great Ape House, and the Helen Brach Primate House. Families meet with the zookeepers to learn about their animals' nighttime habits.

Inside the houses, security lights provide just enough illumination to see what the lions, apes, and primates are up to. In the Lion House, the cats are often very alert and take special interest in watching their visitors. Zookeepers talk about what the animals are usually doing at this late hour.

Throughout the overnighter, zoo staff point out animal behaviors that are revealed at night but invisible by day. Attention is even paid to the nocturnal habits of the rabbits, pigeons, and owls who aren't official residents at the zoo. A program highlight is when a bat expert brings in bats that kids can touch and examine to learn how bats are uniquely adapted to their late-night lifestyle.

Milk and cookies are served at 10:30 P.M. at the Farm-in-the-Zoo, where families can feed the cows, watch the midnight milking, and even try their hand at milking a goat. After returning to the main zoo, families can visit another animal house, watch a nature movie, or turn in. Lights finally go out a few minutes before 2:00 A.M.!

Families sleep near the animals in the Pritzker Children's Zoo. Overnight participants are often as loud as the Children's Zoo animals, which generally settle down in the dark.

After a 6:45 A.M. breakfast and a quiz sheet about the nocturnal adaptations observed during the night, the overnighter ends with an early visit to the McCormick Bird House, where keepers prepare breakfast, clean cages, and otherwise get ready for a new day. Everyone goes home at 8:30 A.M.

The Ark After Dark is offered four times a year to forty people. The cost is $45 per person, $36 for zoo members. Children must be at least 8 years old to attend. For information, contact the Lincoln Park Zoo's Education Department at 742-7692.

Museum of Science and Industry

Still looking for an incentive to join the Museum of Science of Industry? Here's one: its overnight is offered only twice a year, and *only* to members.

Each overnight revolves around a different theme, like the Take Flight Camp-In that celebrated the opening of the *Take*

Flight exhibit in 1994. As families arrived, they were handed ticket folders listing flight-related activities like kite-making and a fold-and-fly paper airplane contest.

The entire museum is open all evening, and sleeping areas can be established anywhere in the museum except the bottom of the coal mine and inside the U505 submarine. It's possible to sleep next to the Boeing 727, in the shadow of the beating heart, or among the space capsules in the Henry Crown Space Center.

With 800 members attending, your family will have lots of friendly company during the evening—yet the exhibits are surprisingly uncrowded. The overnight is your chance to take a private guided tour of the coal mine, or visit the submarine without waiting in line for an hour. You could even spend the whole evening in the Omnimax Theatre, where two features are shown every hour from 8:00 P.M. to midnight. Best of all, everything is free—even exhibits that cost extra during regular museum hours.

A bountiful midnight snack of cookies, Rice Krispie treats, bananas, milk, and juice is served from 10:00 to 11:45 P.M. Museum lights go out at midnight, and continental breakfast is served following the wake-up call (delivered by the coal mine whistle) at 6:30 A.M.

This is an excellent overnight for families with older children. The museum staff takes care to divide activities into two groups, so kids over 13 can work with peers instead of a little brother or sister. And the museum's fantastic range of exhibits holds everyone's attention—even Mom and Dad's.

To attend a Museum of Science and Industry overnight, you must be a museum member, and your children must be at least 7 years old. Admission is $35 for adults, $30 for kids. To join the museum, call the Membership Department at 684-1414.

John G. Shedd Aquarium

Your kids can sleep with the fishes—and live to tell the tale.

Offered two to three times a year to 250 members of the general public, Sleep with the Fishes mixes crafts and educational activities with a special evening marine mammal presentation. The overnight kicks off at 6:00 P.M. with dinner in the Bubblenet, the aquarium's cafe. Soon after, guests enjoy a special performance of the marine mammal presentation in the oceanarium, where dolphins and whales demonstrate some of their natural behaviors.

From 8:00 to 10:00 P.M., families can enjoy educational activities in the Aquatic Education Center. Kids can build orca hats, refine their scrimshaw carving skills, and make fish prints or make architectural rubbings of the aquatic subjects on the aquarium's main brass doors.

At 10:00 P.M., cookies and milk are served next to the coral reef, where guests can talk to the divers feeding its residents. Lights are on until 11:30 P.M., when your family can curl up and rest anywhere in the galleries except the oceanarium.

Continental breakfast is served at 7:00 A.M., when the gift shop opens for early-morning shoppers. The overnight ends at 9:00 A.M.

One caveat: there are no flashlight tours at the aquarium, because flashlights scare the fish. Leave yours at home!

Sleep with the Fishes costs $40 for members, $45 for nonmembers. Children must be at least 8 years old to attend. For information about the next overnight, call the aquarium's Education Department at 939-2426, extension 3420. To make a reservation, call 939-2426, extension 2300.

14

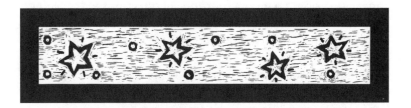

Chicago Behind the Scenes

In a sad footnote to the story of the decline of the Rust Belt, factory tours are becoming a relic of the past. Chicago kids can't watch Sara Lee make enormous vats of brownies because Sara Lee no longer has bakeries in Illinois. They can't see how Tootsie Rolls or Oreo Cookies are made, because liability insurance has forced Tootsie Roll and Nabisco to stop giving plant tours.

But there are some institutions that still roll out the red carpet for kids, classes, and scout troops.

A Tour for Teddy Bear Lovers

At North American Bear's plant on the Near Southwest Side, you can watch the famous VanderBear family being stuffed, dressed, and shipped to well-known toy stores. This tour will be a hit for collectors of the most famous VanderBear, Muffy. The Barbie of the teddy bear set, Muffy has outfits to beat the band, plus Muffy-size furniture and a 22,000-member fan club.

The plant offers free family tours Monday through Friday at 10:30 A.M. during June and August only. (During July, you can arrange a tour through the Chicago Children's Museum, which charges a fee and adds hands-on activities to the plant tour.)

VanderBear fans of all ages love this forty-five-minute tour, so it's a good idea to arrange your visit in the spring. Call the corporate office to reserve a spot and get directions to the factory. Parking is free, and rest rooms are available. Strollers will be accommodated, but North American Bear would rather host children who can walk.

While the tour is free, the teddy bears aren't. To buy a new outfit for Muffy you'll have to visit an upscale toy retailer like F.A.O. Schwarz or North Pier's Enchanted Kingdom.

North American Bear
401 N. Wabash Avenue
329-0020

Take Me Out to the Ballpark

Families are welcome at both of Chicago's baseball stadiums.

Behind-the-scenes tours of Comiskey Park happen every Tuesday and Friday of the year. The ninety-minute tour visits all the public areas, the press box, the swanky Diamond Suites, and the Stadium Club. You'll visit the Sox dugout and look around behind home plate, but you won't get to stand on the field or go in the clubhouse. You'll hear a little about the old ballpark, and lots about the wonders of the new ballpark.

When the Sox are in town, tours are offered at 1:30 P.M.; when no game is scheduled, a 10:30 A.M. tour is also available. Tickets are $5 for adults; $3 for kids. Call the tour hotline at least ten days ahead to make your reservation.

If you want to visit Wrigley Field, plan early. The Cubs organization only gives four tours a year—but they're wonderful. During the ninety-minute tour, your family will explore Wrigley Field from its bottom to top. You'll get a chance to stand on the field, visit the Cubs dugout and the clubhouse for the Cubs and the visiting team, and sit in the press box where Harry Caray sings during the seventh-inning stretch. Your kids will see old photos of past glories, and hear stats galore about players and plays, like Babe Ruth's 500th home run. Not to mention anecdotes about the architecture of the field and the history of the Cubs organization.

Did you know that the field was actually built for a predecessor team called the Whalers, and was known as Weeghman Park until William Wrigley took over? Or that the whole park cost $250,000 to build, while the lights installed in the late eighties cost $13 million? You'll hear plenty of fascinating facts like these, find out the answers to all of your Cubs questions, and get a chance to take all the pictures you want. Why not take your family's Christmas picture on home plate?

A tour of Wrigley Field costs $10; proceeds are donated to Cubs Care. In 1994, the Cubs offered this tour on four dates only. There are plans to increase the number of tours, but it's still a good idea to call early in the spring to reserve your family's place in line.

Chicago Cubs
Wrigley Field
1060 W. Addison Street
404-CUBS

The White Sox
Comiskey Park
333 W. Thirty-fifth Street
Tour hotline: 924-1000, ext. 7182

Extra! Extra! Read All About It!

A tour of the Chicago Tribune's Freedom Center will introduce kids over age 10 to the many steps involved in printing and publishing a major metropolitan daily. Tour guides summarize the editorial process, since the Michigan Avenue editorial offices are not part of the tour, and lead visitors through the third-floor pressroom, where they can see newspaper inserts and the Trib's final market edition being printed.

After visiting the pressroom, the tour moves into the fifth-floor mailing room, where advertising sections are inserted into the paper before it is bundled and sent down to the Tribune delivery trucks.

At the tour's end, all participants receive the Tribune's "20 Famous Headlines Newspaper," a collection of twenty famous (or notorious) front pages bound into a special edition of the paper. Headlines range from the sinking of the *Titanic* and Charles Lindbergh's successful flight to more recent headlines like Michael Jordan's single word headline, "Tremendous."

Forty-five-minute tours are offered Tuesday through Friday at 9:30 A.M., 10:30 A.M., 11:30 A.M., and 1:30 P.M. Children must be over 10 to participate. Reservations are required, but a small family can usually join a tour with less than a week's notice. The tour is wheelchair accessible.

Chicago Tribune Freedom Center
777 W. Chicago Avenue
222-2116

Journalists at Work

If your kids want to see reporters and editors in action, take a tour of the Chicago Sun-Times.

This hour-long tour takes visitors to the newsroom, the pressroom, the composing area, and the sports department. In the newsroom, visitors see editorial staff hard at work on the next day's paper. If the photo editor is free, visitors can see the photo desk and watch pictures coming over the wire. In the sports department, a copy editor is generally available to answer questions about the news-making process and sports news in particular.

In the composing room, kids can see tomorrow's paper being laid out. And in the pressroom, they'll watch the Sun-Times's presses busily printing inserts like the Wednesday food section.

Tours are offered Tuesday, Wednesday, and Thursday at 10:30 A.M. to groups of ten to twenty-five people. The Sun-Times prefers to give tours to kids 12 and up but smaller children will not be turned away. Reserve your tour two to three weeks in advance.

If you want to watch the presses roll without going on a full-blown tour, you can visit the Sun-Times Gallery any weekday from 9:00 A.M. to 5:00 P.M. The Gallery overlooks the pressroom, so kids can look down at the printers and machines going about their business. There's generally an interesting photo display in the Gallery, too.

Chicago Sun-Times
401 N. Wabash Avenue
321-3000
Tour hotline: 321-3251

The World's Biggest Airport

Landing a behind-the-scenes tour of O'Hare Airport takes some planning. Because this tour is not open to individual families, you'll have to arrange a visit for your Cub or Girl Scout troop, school class, or day camp—and then tag along as a chaperone.

But it's worth the effort. This ninety-minute tour reveals the inner workings of the world's busiest airport, from the terminals and the people mover to the service roads and the airport firehouse.

If you arrive in your own van or bus, you'll be escorted onto a service road where your group can watch takeoffs, landings, and other airfield activity. Smaller groups can visit the firehouse and see what preparations have been made for emergencies.

Inside the terminal, your group will learn about O'Hare's history and hear statistics about its phenomenal traffic. The tour guide explains O'Hare's big picture, lighting on specifics like how the airport security system works. Of course, everyone gets to zip around the airport on the sleek but controversial "people mover," stopping for a short visit at the international terminal, where older children will learn about immigration, customs, and other border controls.

Free tours of O'Hare Field are offered Monday through Friday at 10:00 A.M. and 11:30 A.M. to groups of fifteen to forty. (Smaller groups will be paired with another group to make the required minimum.) Participants must be at least 8 years old. Call the number below between 9:00 A.M. and 4:00 P.M. to make reservations at least six weeks in advance.

O'Hare Field Tours
686-2300

Prehistoric Thornton Quarry

Southern Cook County's most amazing spot is the Thornton Quarry. One of the largest commercial stone quarries in the world, the Thornton Quarry is nearly 400 feet deep and contains a supply of marketable stone to last several lifetimes.

It's paradise to Illinois geologists, because it is the largest and richest of the 410-million-year-old fossil reefs unearthed in the Chicago area. It contains a wealth of fossils from the Silurian era, including crinoids, trilobites, brachiopods, and many larger creatures that reached lengths of ten feet.

At one time the Thornton Quarry hosted regular open houses to which the public was invited. Adults can still visit the quarry on field trips conducted by the Chicago Academy of Sciences. But at present, the only way kids under 18 can see it is to drive right up to its edge and peek into its awesome depths.

Fortunately, there's a lot to see from the perimeter. Nine million tons of stone are mined here each year, and it takes a battalion of giant trucks and front-end loaders to loosen and carry stone to a crusher that grinds it into pieces the size of a football. A 3,000-foot conveyor system carries the rock footballs to the processing plant, where they are crushed into various sizes and grades.

Two thousand trucks a day visit the quarry to pick up limestone, aggregates, stone sand, metallurgical stone, and mineral filler. From the edge, they're no bigger than Tonka Trucks, and workers look like tiny figures in a model train layout. But you'll be close enough to feel the earth move when the crew sets off explosives at about 3:00 P.M. weekdays.

To reach a good vantage point, take I-80 to Halsted Street and go south on Halsted to Ridge Road (look for the Fannie Mae

Candy Store). Turn left onto Ridge Road and follow it until you find a spot where you can pull over safely and gaze into the pit through the fence. Call the quarry first to confirm when the crew will be blasting.

Before you make your pilgrimage here, call the Community Relations Department of Material Services Corporation (372-3600), and ask them to send you the informative brochure, "This Is the Thornton Quarry." Written by a geologist, it illustrates the most common types of fossils found in the quarry, and shows what each animal looked like when it was alive. It also talks about the quarry's operation and has pictures of the various earth movers kids will see in action.

You can try requesting permission for a visit by writing to the Community Relations Department, but chances are good your request will be turned down. (Once again, the cost of liability insurance has put an end to regular tours.) If you have a teenager who is over 18, contact the Chicago Academy of Sciences about its tours of the Thornton Quarry. And if you ever, ever get word that the quarry is planning an open house, don't miss it!

Thornton Quarry
183rd and Indiana
Thornton
For blasts schedule, call (708) 877-6540
For permission to visit, write:
Community Relations Department
Material Services Corporation
222 N. LaSalle Drive, Chicago 60601
372-3600

Down at the Bottom of a Hole in the Ground

What happens to water when it goes down the drain? For the answer, visit the Metropolitan Water Reclamation District of Greater Chicago's Deep Tunnel project.

The District has moved the earth more than once in its 105-year history. For starters, it reversed the flow of the Chicago River.

More recently, it is building the $2 billion Deep Tunnel system, which prevents dirty water (or worse, untreated sewage) from entering local waterways during storms.

The tour takes place near Sixty-seventh Street and LaGrange Road in the village of Hodgkins. Inside the Mainstream Pumping Station, visitors watch a twelve-minute movie that explains why the Deep Tunnel project was needed. The station also contains a model pumping station that lets you see its inner workings, and a model of the boring machine that so far has dug sixty-four miles of tunnels through dolomite.

After the movie, an elevator drops you 330 feet to the bottom of the station, where you can see the gigantic 17,500-horsepower pumps that can pump a billion gallons of water in two days. The water is pumped from the tunnel to the nearby treatment plant in Stickney, where 95 percent of all organic pollutants are removed before the water is discharged into streams and rivers that flow away from Lake Michigan. (By the way, the treatment plant is the world's largest.)

Tours of the Deep Tunnel system are offered weekdays only at 10:00 A.M. and 1:00 P.M. to groups of ten or more. Children must be 10 or older to visit, because waste treatment is an abstract process that generally bores younger kids. (Never mind if your kid's a genius; there are no exceptions to this policy.) The tour is free.

Call the District's Public Information Office at 751-6634 for details on how to submit a written request for a tour.

Smashing Cars, Shredding Steel Beams

Industrial recycling *is* exciting—when it's your job to recycle things like stretch limousines and Comiskey Park.

On a tour through Cozzi Recycling, the largest steel recycler in the Midwest, your kids can watch in awe as cars are reduced to compact cubes of steel and enormous steel beams are sliced by a scary pair of hydraulic guillotine shears, aka the scissors that sliced Comiskey.

But how much your kids get to see depends on Frank Cozzi, who personally handles all tour requests. For groups like the Lincoln Park Zoo, which occasionally sponsors family field trips to Cozzi's, the red carpet is rolled out. This deluxe tour includes a movie on industrial recycling, a long-distance look at the car-shredding equipment in action, and an up-close look at the equipment at rest. Visitors see how a car's fluids are captured before it is shredded, how metal is cut and baled, and learn about how recycled metals are used again.

Unlike the Thornton Quarry, you can't watch the goings-on at Cozzi's from the street. From Blue Island Avenue, all your kids can see are the comings and goings of hundreds of old pickups teeming with discarded stoves, bumpers, and refrigerators. (Now you know where that stuff goes when it leaves your alley.) To see it up close, you'll have to put together a group and request a visit. Call Frank Cozzi to arrange your visit a month or two ahead of time. Choose a nice warm, dry month so you won't have to wander through the yard in rain or snow.

You can also try to join the field trip organized by the Lincoln Park Zoo. Call the Education Department (294-4649) to see if and when it has scheduled a field trip to Cozzi.

If you just can't pull off a visit, your kids can watch the action at Cozzi's from the comfort of your own home. Just buy or rent a copy of the children's video, *Crunch, Smash, and Trash*. This Chicago-produced video looks at all aspects of recycling but understandably focuses on Cozzi's dramatic role.

Cozzi Recycling
2232 S. Blue Island Avenue
254-1200

15

Just Plain Fun

Here are some great ideas for days when you want to skip the educational sights and concentrate on fun, fun, fun.

Kohl Children's Museum

Nothing to do on a rainy, school-less day? Head for the Kohl Children's Museum in Wilmette, just a few minutes' drive north of Howard Street.

Arguably the best romper room in town, it holds a fantastic array of activities for children from ages 2 to 10. Parents may find the noise level a little painful, but kids won't run out of things to do. With tabletops groaning under Legos, trays of bubble fluid waiting to be turned into fantastic shapes, everything a kid needs to paint his or her face and dress up for a homemade video, it's hard to think of a better way to spend a morning.

The Kohl Museum is like a treasure chest of props for let's pretend. In Jerusalem: The Old City, kids dress in the costumes of ancient Jerusalem and prepare food, share a meal, visit the *shuk* (the marketplace), or even sit atop the throne in the royal throne room. Young seafarers can enjoy a voyage on the scale-model Phoenician vessel, which boasts a sail that can be raised and lowered, cargo to load, and oars to row.

There are dollhouses, playhouses, a CTA train for young conductors, and best of all, the beloved miniature Jewel

Visitors to the Kohl Children's Museum play on the CTA train in *All Aboard!*, an exhibit that takes children on a realistic train journey through the city of Chicago as it teaches them about train travel. *Photo by the Kohl Children's Museum.*

supermarket. On crowded days (basically all holidays and school vacations) your child may have to wait a few minutes before entering, but it's worth it. No kid can resist loading up a shopping cart and shopping like Mom and Dad! With help, even a 18-month-old can have fun pretending to shop.

Some of the Kohl Museum's exhibits approach more serious issues. *People*, designed to help children understand and celebrate diversity, uses an abundance of games and activities to help children understand racism. One interactive video program features children telling their experiences with racism and asks viewers to consider how they would feel if they experienced the same thing. Another video program teaches kids to dance the Israeli hora, the Irish jig, the Nigerian funga, and other ethnic dances–all while watching themselves dancing on a video screen.

Upstairs in the Art and Technology Center, kids can play keyboards and electric guitars and pump the "wa wa" pedal to their hearts' content. Because they're wearing earphones, the only ears they'll ruin are their own! Scads of art materials–looms, blackboards, paper and crayons, computer-assisted drawing–encourage them to settle down and draw. On the Great Masters' Walls, kids learn a little something about composition by moving around magnetic puzzle pieces to make their own pictures à la van Gogh and Miró.

The Kohl Museum's imaginative special events celebrate major holidays and themes that parents and kids can enjoy together. Mexican Independence Day, for example, is celebrated with Mexican crafts and performances by a Mexican dance troupe. Agatha Christie's birthday is marked with a museum-scale game of Clue. During December, the museum celebrates everything from Hanukkah, Kwanzaa, and Christmas to the Filipino holiday, Cock Crow Mass. In fact, at the Kohl Museum, it's always some kind of holiday!

There's plenty of room for coats and boots, strollers, and diaper bags in the large cloakroom facilities. Both bathrooms offer fold-out changing tables so babies and toddlers can be changed with ease.

During winter and spring school vacations, it's best to arrive early. When attendance surges, the Kohl Museum controls its crowd by selling entrance tickets for 10:00 A.M., 11:00 A.M., and 1:00 P.M.

If you have to wait, or if hunger pangs strike your children, walk next door and eat at **Walker Brothers Pancake House** (153 Green Bay Road, [708] 251-6000). Its friendly staff can efficiently handle parties of any size, and are perfectly willing to accommodate complicated kid requests like chocolate chip pancakes, pigs-in-blankets, or seconds on hot chocolate. Don't be put off by a line at the door. There is usually a fast turnover and chances are good you'll be seated in just a few minutes.

To find out about the Kohl Museum's special events, join the museum, or ask to be placed on its mailing list. As happy recipients of the monthly calendar of events, your kids will never miss any of the fun.

Kohl Children's Museum
165 Green Bay Road
Wilmette
(708) 256-6056

Chicago Children's Museum

At long last, the Chicago Children's Museum migratory years are over. After occupying three spaces in twelve years, it has found a home at Navy Pier. With a ninety-nine-year lease, the museum won't be going anywhere for a long, long time.

And that's good news. Its new home is a bright, colorful, and architecturally ambitious place that goes to great lengths to amuse and educate children. There are three floors of fascinating activities in its quarters at the western end of Navy Pier, where the windows of the Great Hall offer a stunning view of the city.

The new museum incorporates all the old favorite exhibits— the *City Hospital*, the *Art and Science of Bubbles*, *the Stinking Truth about Garbage*, and the cozy *Touchy Business*, where little kids can crawl through tunnels, cook in a miniature kitchen, pretend to drive, and otherwise enjoy themselves in a calm, carpeted area off-limits to big kids. Also carried over from the old quarters is the working television studio, where kids can take turns delivering news and weather, running the camera, or directing a segment.

To celebrate its new, nautical location, the museum has a waterworks exhibit, and its enormous climbing schooner encourages imaginative play and develops motor skills. The new *Under Construction* exhibit gives kids a chance to tackle real construction problems with real tools and materials. With the help of a docent, kids can use hammers and saws to build kid-sized furniture, forts, and other projects.

Inventing: the Process of Discovery teaches basic scientific principles and showcases the inventions of young people. The adjacent Inventing Lab lets kids do a little inventing of their own—including making their own music on the enormous music machine.

In the Art Abounds studio, kids can stop and make quick art projects or participate in a longer, more structured class. The studio is full of materials to stimulate the imagination and is often attended by an artist-in-residence who leads kids in art projects in all media. Outside the studio is a gallery where art by adults is never shown: it only showcases the creativity and talent of children!

The museum offers many special events on weekends and on Thursday nights, when the museum is free. These drop-in workshops generally tie into the museum's exhibits, so your kids can make rain sticks near the rain forest exhibit, or study a worm farm in the recycling area, or participate in a make-and-take art program in the art studio or Touchy Business area.

In its new location, the museum continues to offer its popular City Stalker Day Camp program for kids ages 5 to 12. This program revolves around field trips that introduce kids to various neighborhoods and institutions. Accompanied by counselors, kids travel to their destinations by bus and el. Destinations generally relate to the week's overall theme. In News Stalkers, for example, kids visit local television stations, meet real reporters, and produce their own video or print news report of their week. While the museum has expanded, the enrollment for City Stalkers is limited. Sign up in February to make sure your kids can attend.

The Chicago Children's Museum is open Tuesday through Sunday from 10:00 A.M. to 4:30 P.M. Admission is $3.50 for adults

and $2.50 for children, but Thursdays from 5:00 to 8:00 P.M. the
museum is free to all.

Chicago Children's Museum
600 E. Grand Avenue
527-1000

Navy Pier:
Carnival by the Lake

For years a collection of shabby warehouses, Navy Pier blossomed
into a great family destination in the summer of 1995. Anchored
at one end by the new Chicago Children's Museum and at the
other by the beautiful Grand Ballroom, the pier offers a wonderful
place for a lakeside stroll and an afternoon of activities.

During the summer, the pier has almost a carnival atmosphere,
thanks to the merry-go-round and the Ferris wheel—the only such
permanent structures in Chicago. The gorgeous musical carousel,
which has thirty-six custom-made menagerie horses,
commemorates the twenties, when another merry-go-round
twirled around the pier. The fifteen-story-tall Ferris wheel
dominates the skyline and gives your family a thrilling view of
Chicago's dramatic lakefront.

Along the pier's south dock, there are plenty of places to enjoy
a waterside meal. You can carry out fast food, or savor a sit-down
meal in one of the restaurants overlooking the dock.

Free trolleys carry you up and down the pier if you're too
tired to walk. When it's cold, you can stroll the length of the
pier along the heated, glass-enclosed walkway. Don't miss the
Crystal Gardens, where 32,000 square feet of lush, tended indoor
botanical gardens (seventy-five palm trees—count 'em!) offer the
perfect respite from a dark, cold winter. The gardens are
punctuated by a series of computer-controlled fountains that
are programmed to make the water look like glass-tubed archways.

Navy Pier's large-screen IWERKS theater creates a bigger-than-
life viewing experience. Many of the films shown here have

nautical or nature themes, to celebrate the Pier's distinguished maritime history.

Admission to Navy Pier is free, but the merry-go-round, Ferris wheel, IWERKS theater, and Chicago Children's Museum all levy separate entrance fees.

Navy Pier
600 E. Grand Avenue
595-PIER (7437)

North Pier Festival Marketplace

You could easily spend a day with your kids at North Pier Festival Marketplace. But if you do, bring your wallet.

This old brick warehouse turned mall is home to many marvelous attractions reviewed elsewhere in this book, like Virtuality and the Bicycle Museum of America. It also boasts a miniature golf course and interesting shops like the Hologram Store, where you can "ooh" and "aah" over holograms of tigers that roar, sharks that lunge, and clowns that wink. (Kids under 15 must be accompanied by adults.)

On weekends, visitors can enjoy the antics of the North Pier Performing Troupe. These fifteen jugglers, clowns, mimes, and face painters wander through the marketplace twisting balloons, painting faces, and generally amusing kids. North Pier's mascot, Augie the friendly dinosaur, also works the weekend crowd.

When you're hungry, the basement food court offers standards like Sbarros, Subway, and McDonald's Express, plus a unique dessert spot called the Fudgery, where fudge makers yuk it up with the crowds and pass out plenty of free samples.

For a sit-down meal, try Lettuce Entertain You's Original A-1 Barbecue. On Friday, Saturday, and Sunday, kids can enjoy a special grazing table piled with Tater Tots, Jell-O, peanut butter and jelly quesadillas, and many more wonderful side dishes and desserts. Skip the Baja Beach Club and Dick's Last Resort, both of which lure singles with cheesy props like dangling brassieres.

North Pier Festival Marketplace
401-465 E. Illinois Street
836-4300
(800) FUN-PIER

High-tech Gaming

If your kids like Nintendo and other high-tech games, don't miss the third floor of North Pier at Virtual World, a collection of video and virtual reality games for video fans of all ages.

Depending on your point of view, this noisy peek at gaming of the future will excite you or depress you, which makes this a thought-provoking outing for those who want to muse on the phenomenon of video gaming as they guide their kids through this astonishing maze of lights, noise, and action.

This entertainment complex is divided into four areas: two virtual reality sections, a laser tag area, and a video game arcade. Skip the entire complex if you have very small children, or limit their visit to a ride in the mechanical car in the hallway. If you have elementary-age kids or teens, they will probably run first to the video arcade, Time-Out Entertainment, where dozens of quarter-eating machines let them steer motorcycles and cars into unbelievable accidents, or shoot at movie-quality bad guys in a cowboy bar. In the midst of games that reward your kids for dangerous driving and deadly marksmanship are a few nonviolent, almost old-fashioned games like air hockey. But by and large, this arcade is sure to trigger a headache, just as carnivals made *your* parents grab the Excedrin.

Preteens and teens will enjoy the laser tag game Cyberia, in which ten kids—divided into two teams—are fitted out with laser headgear and laser guns and ushered into a darkened, smoke-filled room. You can watch them track each other down through the plate glass window, if you can make out your kids through the smoke.

There are long lines for this ten-minute game, so if your kids want to play, buy tickets ($5) before you move to the video arcade. They will be assigned a game time and paged when it's their turn to play. Parents of asthmatics, beware! A sign posted outside the game chamber warns that asthmatics and others who are sensitive to smoke should not play this game.

Grown-ups and some teens will want to play the virtual reality games, which cost $4 for four minutes. Those who haven't played video games will be cannon fodder (or is it laser fodder?), but it's worth $4 just to experience this. To play Dactyl Terror, for example, you stand in an elevated podium, don a belt, and a gun-shaped joy stick equipped with two buttons—one to make you walk, one to shoot. The attendant encloses you in a large metal ring, covers your head with a "visette" that projects the video battlefield in front of you, and launches the game.

Suddenly you're walking around a landscape that looks like an M. C. Escher painting in four colors: staircases lead nowhere, columns support nothing, edges drop into oblivion. As you push the button that makes you walk, you use your whole body to turn left and right, looking up and down and behind you for deadly pterodactyls who will attack you. You can hide behind pillars, seek shelter under arches, take aim behind walls. When a pterodactyl "kills" you, a tiny human figure tumbles through endless space and shatters at the bottom of a pit. You fall right behind him, but after you've shattered, you're right back in the game.

It's four amazing minutes even if you never get the hang of it and end up shooting all the wrong targets. Watching the players while you wait your turn is amazing, too. As they move in response to video stimuli, they seem to be performing weird solo dances conducted to music no one can hear.

Young adults—mostly males in their twenties—are the ones flocking to play these games, but a teen who knows Nintendo will probably want to play a few rounds. Really sophisticated players can step across the hallway to BattleTech, "the world's first digital theme park," where a twenty-five-minute round of BattleTech or Red Planet costs $9.

Each adventure begins with a ten-minute briefing session that shows you the basics of virtual reality warfare. Then you enter a virtual reality pod and spend ten minutes battling "battlemechs," futuristic two-legged mercenary tanks that "drift from planet to planet fighting for whoever offers the most cash." After the fighting ends you get a five-minute play-by-play recap of the battle's highlights and a souvenir pilot's log of your adventure.

Like video games, these virtual reality games can be played at a variety of skill levels. But at $9 a pop, it's an expensive habit. And on weekends, advance reservations (call first) are a necessity to avoid a two-hour wait for a "launch."

An afternoon at Virtual World will be exhilarating but expensive, especially if you are hosting several kids, paying for parking at North Pier, and planning to treat everyone to the food court afterward. A cheaper approach is to play one or two games and then watch the overhead video screens to see what each virtual reality player is experiencing. Cheapest of all is to watch the screens without ever playing—an ideal approach for anyone intrigued by this brave new world of entertainment, but not ready to commit to it.

Cyberia, Time-Out, and Virtuality are open Monday through Thursday from 11:00 A.M. to 10:00 P.M. Weekend hours are much, much longer: Friday from 11:00 A.M. to 1:00 A.M., Saturday from 10:00 A.M. to 2:00 A.M., and Sunday from 11:00 A.M. to 8:00 P.M.

Battletech is open Monday to Thursday from 11:00 A.M. to 11:00 P.M., Friday and Saturday from 10:00 A.M. to 1:00 P.M., and Sunday from 10:00 A.M. to 11:00 P.M.

BattleTech, Cyberia, Time-Out, and Virtuality
North Pier Festival Market
435 E. Illinois Street
BattleTech: 836-5977
Cyberia, Time-Out, and Virtuality: 527-3002

One Kid's Day In Cyberspace

My experience with virtual reality was pretty incredible. When I got there, I was pretty excited, because I didn't know what it would be like. To tell you the truth, I was scared.

When we came in, we saw a TV screen that told us how to put on the equipment. Then we had to choose a game. Most people think that all the games contain violence, but some don't. They have VR games for little kids, too, so they won't be left out. We chose Dactyl Nightmare, the easiest and cheapest game. Our tickets came with a number on the back to tell you when your turn comes. Don't worry, they will yell it out. It's like the countdown to the unknown.

Once our number was called I was really scared. The people who work there put the equipment on us and the game started. It turned out that the game wasn't scary after all and was actually fun. I really recommend this game for the whole family. It's very competitive.

If you decide that you don't want to play a virtual reality game, there is an arcade and laser tag on the same floor. Try it out. You'll love it.

—Michael White
Edgewater

Photon

Hidden away on 171st and Halsted Streets behind the Holiday Inn is one of my favorite things to do on the South Side. n fact, it's one of my favorite things to do anywhere on the planet. Photon. Photon (17140 Halsted Street, Harvey, [708] 331-4263) is one of the best-kept secrets around. Photon is a lot like war games played in forest preserves, except you use laser-light guns instead of paint pellets.

Laser-light guns may sound kind of extreme, but they merely register "hits" on the light-sensitive helmets and chest plates everyone wears. The object is to shoot the other team before they shoot you. If you get hit, your equipment powers down for a few seconds. All of the helmets, guns, and chest targets are connected electronically, and scores are tallied by computer.

In my several Photon trips, I've seen all kinds of people there, although if you go at night, expect to see a lot of teenage club hoppers. Photon has also been the site for several Electronic Bulletin Board gatherings, so watch out for computer nerds like me. The price is two or three dollars per game with discounted packages for three and more games. For my money, however, the best deal is the all-day unlimited play ticket for $10 dollars.

Little kids may feel a little overwhelmed, but most older kids (8 or 9 and up, including their parents), will have a great time. Happy hunting!

–Roman Zabicki
Chicago Lawn

Roller-Skating

At the Rainbo Roller Rink you and your kids can skate to the beat of high-volume hip-hop. A pulsing light show, great music, tasty pizza, and Cokes—roller-skating doesn't get much better than this. And during the afternoon family sessions, you can still do the hokey-pokey with the dino-on-wheels master of ceremonies, the Skateasaurus.

A smaller, separate rink for beginners is a nice feature of this family-oriented rink, which is a great treat after school or during school vacations. Call for a schedule of sessions for younger skaters. The Fleetwood Roller Rink is its South Side counterpart.

Rainbo Roller Rink
4836 N. Clark Street
271-6200

Fleetwood Roller Rink
7231 S. Archer Avenue
Summit
(708) 458-0300

Batting Cages, Miniature Golf, and Ice Cream

Yep—three good reasons to spend an afternoon at Novelty Golf in Lincolnwood!

Aspiring ball players can practice slugging at Novelty Golf's large outdoor batting cages. A dollar gets you eighteen pitches in a slow, medium, or fast cage or one of the two softball cages. When the batting cage gets boring, shuffle on over to the miniature golf course, where a game ranges from $2.75 per person weekdays to $5.75 per person on weekends. And when that gets dull, your kids will be just steps away from the Bunny Hutch, famous purveyor of hot dogs, hamburgers, and soft ice-cream cones dipped in chocolate. You can relax under the umbrella-covered outdoor tables, or enjoy your cones while critiquing the skills of other ballplayers.

Novelty Golf's batting cages and miniature golf range are open from April to October.

Novelty Golf
3640 W. Devon Avenue
Lincolnwood
(708) 679-9434

Rock Climbing in Chicago

Rock climbing is perfect for the adventuresome and energetic young kid. It's great exercise and a lot better than playing video games or watching TV.

There are two indoor rock climbing facilities in Chicago. Gravity Indoor-Outdoor Climbing Wall (1935 S. Halsted Street, 733-5006) and Hidden Peak

(937 W. Chestnut Street, 536-9400) which is located in the same building as Lakeshore Gymnastics.

Both gyms rent gear for $10 to $20, including your entrance fee. If you have gear, the cost is only $5 to $10 for two hours—but who's timing it? Some gyms offer lessons and some have competitions every once in a while for more skilled climbers.

There are not many great outdoor climbing places outdoors near Chicago; the closest is three hours away. That is why gyms are important. If climbing is done safely, it is a great sport but these safety precautions must be taken:

- Check harness and all gear

- Replace old gear when needed

- Don't climb without rope

- Always climb with at least a couple other people

—Willie McBride
Andersonville

The Chicago Park District

Never mind its scandalous past and rumors of its shady practices. Thanks to the Chicago Park District, the city's families have an abundance of recreational opportunities—most of them absolutely free. From indoor and outdoor ice-skating to gymnastics and swimming classes, inexpensive year-round toddler programs and summer day-camp programs, supervised public beaches and playgrounds, and organized athletic teams, the Chicago Park District offers so many programs for kids that it deserves a guidebook of its own.

And finally, there is one! To make it easier for Chicago families to find out about its programs, the Park District publishes an annual directory of all parks and their programs. In this guide, you'll find the name, address, phone number, and programs of every Chicago park, plus a listing of the District's six regions. Each region also publishes a seasonal directory of activities in each of its parks.

To request a copy of the District's catalog, call 747-2200. To get a regional schedule of activities, call your regional office:

- Central Region: Garfield Park, 100 N. Central Park Avenue, 747-7640

- Lakefront Region: South Shore Cultural Center, 7059 S. South Shore Drive, 747-2474

- Near North Region: Riis Park, 6221 W. Wrightwood Avenue, 746-5357

- North Region: Warren Park, 6601 N. Western Avenue, 742-7879

- South Region: Kennicott Park, 4434 S. Lake Park Avenue, 747-7661

- Southwest Region: Foster Park, 1440 W. Eighty-fourth Street, 747-6136

At the local level, most of the 600 Park District facilities in Chicago publish a printed schedule of programs and activities. To find out about programs in your area, check with the parks closest to you. If your local park doesn't offer what you are looking for, chances are good its employees can tell you how to find it. But if you're completely at a loss, go to the top. The Park District's Communication Department (294-2493) will do its best to match you with the right program.

16

Kid Food

Arugula and fettucine may enchant *your* palate, but kids still go for hot dogs, hamburgers, french fries, pizza, and ice cream.

Hot Dogs and Hamburgers

Part of the successful McDonald's formula is to design restaurants and menus that look pretty much the same no matter where you are.

Definitely not part of the formula is the **Rock-n-Roll McDonald's**, where life-size statues of the Beatles greet you as you enter, and the soundtrack is sixties rock 'n' roll.

This McDonald's, said to be one of the busiest in the world, offers an exciting jumble of juke boxes, shiny Naugahyde booths, old Beatles pictures and other memorabilia from the fifties and sixties.

In this museum of pop culture, you can tell your kids all about old heartthrobs like the Beatles, the Monkees, Elvis, and James Dean. There's something to look at and remember every minute of your meal. Even kids who could care less about their parents' music can't resist the appeal of this place!

Rock-n-Roll McDonald's is located at 600 N. Clark Street (664-7940).

Friendly, blinking mascots welcome families to Superdawg Drive-in, modeled after the Midway Airport control tower. *Courtesy Superdawg Drive-in.*

Byron's and **Fluky's** are two North Side hot dog institutions that go out of their way to accommodate children. **Fluky's** is fun to visit any time, but the ornate Hanukkah and Christmas displays make the winter holidays a special time to visit. **Byron's** is an outer space wonderland bursting with colorful three-dimensional space rockets and space creatures that are even more spectacular than the hot dogs. Fluky's is located at 6821 N. Western (274-3652); the outer space Byron's is at 6016 N. Clark (973-5000).

Remember when drive-ins, not drive-throughs, stood on every corner of suburban America? Give your kids a taste of the good old days by visiting **Superdawg Drive-in** at 6363 N. Milwaukee Avenue at Devon (763-0660).

You can eat in your car at this bona fide Chicago landmark, a replica of the Midway Airport Control Tower. Carhops attach a tray of hot dogs and onion rings to your car window, so you can savor your food and the panoramic view of Milwaukee Avenue at the same time. When you're done, let your kids switch on the red light. Presto! Your carhop will return to sweep away the debris and collect a tip. To grown-ups, it's a pretty sentimental experience. To a kid, it's way cool.

When the Train Comes Along

Younger children will be delighted by **The Choo Choo Restaurant**, at 600 Lee Street, in Des Plaines ([708] 298-5949) and **Snackville Junction**, 9144 S. Kedzie Avenue, in Evergreen Park ([708] 423-1313), where lunch comes to them on a train!

Both restaurants feature a nifty little model train whose tracks circle the main counter and adjacent booths. When an order comes up, baskets of sandwiches and fries are balanced atop the flat cars, and the scrappy engine pulls the meal around to your child. (Drinks and other tippy items are delivered by a waitress.)

Both restaurants serve standard snack shop fare: hot dogs, hamburgers, grilled cheese sandwiches, french fries, sodas, and malts. For the best view, sit at the counter, so your tot can watch the busy train go around and around making its deliveries. With all eyes glued to the train, lunch at one of these diners may be the calmest meal you've had in a long time.

Real Restaurants

Take a step back in time at **Ed Debevic's**, the gleaming, artifact-filled retro diner at 640 N. Wells Street (664-1707).

A meal at Ed's is a full-scale experience. Kids love Ed's spirited waiters and waitresses, who wear tongue-in-cheek costumes and engage in all kinds of nonsense. Your waitperson may be dressed like a paratrooper, a Boy Scout, or a nurse. She may be wearing a fifties prom gown or a poodle skirt; he may be decked out as a cowboy, ready to draw plastic pistols on request. On one visit, lucky diners were served by the Mr. Clean of commercials of yore: snow white T-shirt and pants, bulging upper arms, shaved head, fake bushy eyebrows, and a belt dripping with feather dusters, squirt bottles, and other cleaning paraphernalia.

Bantering with the servers is part of the fun. Expect your family to be sassed, teased, admonished, and cajoled while you order, while you wait, and while you eat. Food comes fast and time flies quickly thanks to the countless signs to read, kitsch to admire, and cultural details to explain to kids who missed the fifties and sixties. And there's music: "Shimme Shimme Cocoa Puff," "Leader of the Pack," "Stop! In the Name of Love"—all tunes that lift sagging spirits and make you want to dance in the aisle.

Menu prices range from $2.95 to $6 for hot dogs and hamburgers, fries, malts and milkshakes, meatloaf, and other diner fare. To avoid the lunch and dinner crowds, go a little early or a little late: try wrapping up a day of downtown adventures with a meal at 4:30 P.M., and you'll get a table with no wait at all.

For dinner alfresco—in an indoor forest of fruit trees—head for **foodlife**, Lettuce Entertain You's take on the food court concept. Instead of hot dogs on a plastic tray, your kids can enjoy healthful, delicious food in surroundings that delight kids and parents.

When you enter the forest you are given a plastic ticket that records your purchases, and guided to a red-checked table under one of the lighted artificial trees. Atop the table is an ingenious flip chart that tells waiters when you need help. To reserve your table, flip to a sign that tells the wait staff you're getting food, then head out to graze among the stir-fry delights, fresh pizza and pasta, and low-fat desserts.

If your kid spills her water, flip the sign to We Need Help. Someone will be right over to assist you. When you're ready to go, flip the sign to Bill Please, and your check will be presented in minutes.

The food is great, the atmosphere is fine, the mechanics of the little signs are fascinating. All in all, foodlife is a pretty good family night out! Foodlife is located on the mezzanine at Water Tower Place, 835 N. Michigan Avenue (335-3663).

"Kids can run like monsters at **Ricobene's**," says one southside mother of four. This food emporium falls about halfway between a sit-down restaurant and a cafeteria. You place your order at a counter, but it's brought to your table by a waitress—in record time. Decorated with old posters of fifties horror movies and old memorabilia from Chicago institutions like Riverview, it's colorful, fast, huge (there's never any waiting), and a pretty good deal for families. A la carte items like spaghetti with meat sauce, chili, chicken Vesuvio, or hamburgers cost between $3 and $5; salads, vegetables, and desserts are priced separately. If Ricobene's fast service isn't fast enough for your starving horde, skip the dining and use the drive-through!

Ricobene's is at 8231 S. Cicero Avenue (581-6530).

Food and Magic

Two Chicago institutions treat your kids to a magic show over dinner.

The family-friendly **Leona's** chain offers tabletop magic at all five locations. On weekends, magicians meander from table to table, performing amazing tricks and making fabulous balloon animals for the little ones. Performance hours vary, so call Leona's catering office (292-4312) to find out when the magic starts at the location nearest you.

Besides tabletop magic, Leona's offers toy-, game-, and cartoon-filled kids' rooms at its Oak Park and Augusta Boulevard restaurants. Kids can hang out in the room until dinner is ready, or even eat there while Mom and Dad enjoy a meal alone. (Teenage attendants keep an eye on things in your absence.) The kid's menu dishes up kid-sized portions of cheese pizza, chicken, pasta, turkey sandwiches, and other favorites.

Leona's restaurants are located at 3215 N. Sheffield Avenue (327-8861), 6935 N. Sheridan Road (764-5757), 1936 W. Augusta Boulevard (292-4300), 1419 W. Taylor Street (850-2222), and 848 W. Madison Street in Oak Park ([708] 445-0101).

Schulien's Restaurant and Saloon has been owned by magicians for four generations. At least one of those generations is responsible for a piece of twentieth-century popular culture. According to local magicians, patriarch Matt Schulien added carrots carved in the shape of goldfish to his fish bowl. To amuse his guests, he would pull the carrot out from among the live fish, shake it out, and swallow it.

Like all magic tricks, it was an illusion. But college-age patrons didn't know—and thus was born the live goldfish-swallowing craze of the twenties.

Today, patrons are more likely to swallow a good German dinner than real or pretend goldfish. The reasonably priced dinners are heavy on meat and potatoes; dessert is hot apple strudel.

With white tablecloths, muted lighting, and real glass and china, this place calls for manners. The payoff comes after dinner, when a Schulien's magician (perhaps Charlie or Bobby, Matt's son and grandson) spends ten minutes performing tabletop magic for you. During the performance, squeals of delight are perfectly appropriate.

Schulien's is located at 2100 W. Irving Park Road in Chicago (478-2100).

Food and Pageantry

If your kids are enthralled by the notion of knights in armor, spend an evening at the **Medieval Times Dinner and Tournament Castle** in suburban Schaumburg, where dinner is a reenactment of an eleventh-century medieval banquet.

As you and your family eat your way through roast chicken and ribs, you'll be treated to a two-hour tournament in which six knights on horseback spar with one another in medieval games, sword fights, and jousting matches. The horses are real: the dinner tables surround an enormous arena where all the action takes place.

Before dinner, your kids can visit with the horses or wander through the grotesque displays in the torture chamber museum. And of course there's a gift shop, stocked with plenty of medieval-type souvenirs to take home.

You'll have to make reservations to see the tournament, but only a couple of days ahead. Sometimes it's possible to get reservations on the same day. Prices are steep, but considering the size of the meal (it comes with lots of wine and beer for the grown-ups, and soda for the kids) and the scope of the entertainment, you get a lot of bang for your buck.

Dinner performances are offered Wednesday through Saturday evenings and Sunday afternoons. Children under 2 are free if they sit on your lap; kids ages 2 through 12 are $22.75, and adults pay $30 on weeknights and $37.25 on weekends. On

Wednesday and Thursday, dinner begins at 7:30 P.M.; on Friday and Saturday, at 8:00 P.M.. If your kids have an early bedtime, try the 4:00 P.M. dinner on Sunday. Medieval Times Dinner and Tournament Castle is located at the intersection of Roselle Road and Northwest Tollway in Schaumburg ([708] 843-3900).

Blue Plate Specials for Growing Teens

The best way to feed a starving teen is to treat them to dinner at a Polish buffet. Second and third helpings are encouraged at these culinary gems, where the whole family can eat for peanuts.

Near Belmont and Milwaukee is the **Red Apple**, where the telephone is answered in Polish, you'll be greeted in Polish, and the families and workers dining with you will speak Polish. The Red Apple's steam table groans under the weight of pierogi, *nalishniki*, potato pancakes, pork chops, chicken, beans, red cabbage, salad, and dessert. Before 4:00 P.M., the buffet dinner costs $4.89; after 4:00 the price leaps to $5.98. (The Saturday and Sunday buffet offers more and better meat; the price is $6.32.) Beer and soda are extra and prices are somewhat lower for children under 10.

The Red Apple Restaurant (*Czerwone Jabko* in Polish; sounds like "shadvoneh yiapkoh" when they answer the phone) is located at 3123 N. Milwaukee Avenue (588-5781).

Down on the Southwest Side, the nightly buffet at the **Tatra Inn** surrounds a meat selection like prime rib or roast crown of pork with piles of Polish and traditional American side dishes. Here's what $6.95 will get you on a Thursday night: barbecued pork ribs, croquettes, roast beef, roasted chicken, polish sausage, fruit dumplings, potato pancakes, sauerkraut, rice, stuffed cabbage, steamed vegetables, salads, appetizers, fresh fruits, homemade pastries, hot blintzes, homemade soup (including czarina or tripe), and dinner rolls and butter.

The price goes up to $10.45 on Friday, when New York strip steak, chilled shrimp, and Alaskan snow crab legs are featured;

the $9.25 Saturday and Sunday dinners also include more expensive meats.

Kids 4 and under eat at the Tatra for $2.50; kids 5 to 10 pay $5. An inexpensive lunch buffet is also available. The Tatra Inn is at 6040 S. Pulaski Road (582-8313).

Ice Cream

Friendly, family-oriented **Zephyr Ice Cream Parlor** at 1777 W. Wilson Avenue (728-6070) serves up giant creations like the Titanic in a neon blue art deco interior that pulses with energy on the weekends, when Ravenswood teenagers make it "date central." Zephyr's staff is always happy to push together tables for big groups like soccer or swim teams celebrating a victory. **Petersen's Ice Cream**, 1100 Chicago Avenue in Oak Park ([708] 306-6131) offers more modest-sized ice-cream creations in its Victorian-style parlor across the street from Frank Lloyd Wright's striking homes. Don't miss the hot fudge!

Two ice-cream stores serve their sinful creations with a taste of times past. The homemade treats at **Gertie's Own Ice Cream Parlor** have been a Chicago Lawn institution since it opened in 1920. From its red velvet booths you can admire an impressive collection of enormous stuffed bears and unicorns, plus autographed photos of Ann Jillian and other celebrities. If you need a hot meal, order some Gertie's chili—or go straight for the dessert menu and try the Tummy Buster, a giant ice-cream soda served with Gertie's homemade whipping cream. Also delicious are the frozen bananas, Gertie's homemade candy, and Gertie's homemade root beer, available in liters you can take home. Gertie's is at 5858 S. Kedzie Avenue (737-7634).

A year younger but very similar in spirit is **Margie's Candies**, 1960 N. Western Avenue (384-1035). Like Gertie's place, Margie's is much treasured by camera crews looking for interiors that evoke a more genteel era. Margie serves sodas, shakes, phosphates, and ice-cream creations like her turtle sundae, slathered in fudge and caramel sauces made in her kitchen. Margie's ice cream is literally served on the half shell in ceramic shell dishes that range from ladylike to gigantic. And she'll give you a free box of candy if you can prove it's your birthday!

There's only one minor drawback: kids have to be polite when they visit Margie's. If they can read, they'll pick up on that themselves from the signs posted around the restaurant that glower, "Children must remain seated with an adult at all times." No running here!

For an unusual treat, try a Rainbow Cone from **Rainbow Cone**, 9233 S. Western Avenue (238-7075) in Chicago's Beverly neighborhood. This cone is topped with slabs of five different flavors of ice cream: chocolate, strawberry, Palmer House (described by an employee as "a Venetian vanilla with walnuts and cherries"), green pistachio, and orange sherbet. Devotees swear there's nothing like it—and it's been on the menu for sixty-eight years.

There is no indoor seating at Rainbow Cone. There are a few tables outside, but most people eat their Rainbow Cones in their cars.

Thanks to its new Union Station location, Rainbow Cone is now slightly more convenient to north- and northwestsiders. If Beverly is too far out of your way, just look for Rainbow Cone in the mezzanine food court at Union Station, Jackson and Canal Streets (876-2663).

17

Powwows, Parties, and Parades
A Seasonal Guide to Fun

Ever hear about the perfect winter school vacation activity after vacation is over, and then forget about it the next year until it's too late once again?

Keep this chapter near at hand, and you'll have a year's worth of ideas at your fingertips to celebrate seasons, Saturdays, and holidays with your kids!

Winter

Your family can either embrace winter in Chicago, or try to escape it. A good way to throw yourselves into winter is by visiting the Forest Preserve District of Cook County's January **Winter Festival**. At the festival, your family can toboggan to its heart's content, enjoy a horse-drawn sleigh ride through the woods, or sip hot chocolate as an ice sculptor creates a masterpiece from a huge block of ice—all absolutely free. There are also nature scavenger hunts, winter skill demonstrations, and craft activities, puppet shows, and close encounters with roaming polar bears and penguins. ([708] 771-1014)

If your kids have never gone cross-country skiing, pack your family off to one of Camp Sagawau's **Family Weekends**, when kids 8 to 11 can master basic skiing skills through entertaining games and activities. When the lessons are over, stay for the afternoon nature ski through the quiet forest. ([708] 257-2045)

When your kids *can* stand up on skis, spend a Saturday night in the woods! The February **Moonlight Ski** at Deer Grove Forest Preserve lets you ski under the stars on a path illuminated by candles, enjoy the beauty of the forest after dark, and warm up with a cup of wine or hot chocolate by a roaring bonfire. ([708] 771-1014)

Itching for winter to end? Wander over to the Brookfield Zoo's **Groundhog Day** party and watch the zookeepers use special treats to lure their resident groundhogs out of their cozy lairs. Whether they appear or not, your family can enjoy special refreshments near the little critters. ([708] 485-0263)

In February, visit the Oriental Institute on **Discover Nubia! Day**, an all-ages celebration of African American History Month and the culture of ancient Nubia. Once a fierce rival of the ancient Egyptians, the vanished Nubians thrived in what today is southern Egypt and northern Sudan. Festivities at the museum include films, gallery talks, crafts, and games. A highlight in the past has been the reenactment of a traditional Nubian wedding ceremony by member of the Nubian Cultural Center in Toronto. This spectacle of music and movement is a wonderful way to experience the riches of Africa. (702-9514)

Presidents' Day is a perfect day for a civic lesson—especially when it takes place at the Chicago Historical Society. In the morning, kids can participate in a presidential game, design their own national currency, or write a letter to the president. After lunch, actors reenact the Lincoln-Douglas debate and portray Harriet Beecher Stowe and other Civil War–era dignitaries. It's a great way to bring U.S. history to life for school-age kids! (642-4600)

Spring

Spring is a great time for circuses, when the **Shriner's Circus** rolls into the big top at the Medinah Temple (600 N. Wabash Avenue, 266-5000). The Shriner's Circus lacks the high-voltage special effects of Ringling Brothers Barnum & Bailey or the Cirque de Soleil, but it makes up for it by providing an intimacy that is lost in larger venues. No child will be very far from the action in the center ring. A bonus is its accessibility: volunteer Shriners will go out of their way to help disabled kids get in and out and use the Temple's facilities. Round out your visit to the circus with a trip to the Rock-n-Roll McDonald's on Clark Street.

Kids can go hog-wild on **Pig Day**, the Brookfield Zoo's March 1 celebration of our fine swine friends. A special pig movie runs throughout the afternoon (sometimes it's E. B. White's classic, *Charlotte's Web*), and kids can visit and learn more about Brookfield's pig residents Oreo and Tango. As Oreo and Tango munch their dinner, kids can pig out on cake, swill lemonade, and compete in an old-fashioned pig-calling contest. ([708] 485-0263)

During the Frank Lloyd Wright Home and Studio's **April Lego Days**, you and your kids can help build a city out of a half ton of Legos. The Home and Studio helpfully provides an infrastructure of roads and a few basic buildings, but otherwise kids are free to add any structure they please: a home, a hospital, a fire station, a skyscraper, even a space station! Real architects are on hand to provide advice on thorny questions of structure and design. ([708] 848-1500)

If your kids love magic, watch for the **IBM Ring 43 Annual Magic Show**. Ring 43, the local chapter of the International Brotherhood of Magicians, showcases eight different professional magicians in each year's show. Tickets for this festival of sleight-of-hand can be purchased at Magic, Inc. (5082 N. Lincoln Avenue, 334-2855). Chicago's premier magic store, it sells hundreds tricks and accessories like magic stands and ventriloquist dummies. It also acts as a clearinghouse for Chicago magicians, whose performances are posted on the bulletin board. If you're looking for a show to attend, a magician for a party, or a private tutor for your magic-hungry kid, you'll find the contacts you want here. Magic, Inc. also promotes the Southside Magic Masters annual spring dinner and show, when magicians perform table tricks during dinner and mount a platform show afterward.

There are lots of great ways to celebrate Easter in Chicago. Have **Breakfast with Mr. and Mrs. Bunny** at the Brookfield Zoo ([708] 485-0263), **decorate ceramic eggs** at Kids and Clay (878-5821), or attend a **Lithuanian egg decorating class** at the Balzekas Museum of Lithuanian Culture (582-6500). Treat your kids to a fantastic array of chocolate bunnies, lamb cakes, and pastries shaped like rabbits, chicks, and bunny faces at the Lutz Pastry Shop and Cafe (2458 W. Montrose Avenue, 478-7785), where you can shop for Easter basket goodies until 10:00 P.M. during Easter week.

Celebrate **Passover** at the Spertus Museum, where your kids can work with a professional potter to sculpt and fire a ceramic Seder plate. (922-9012)

Summer

Kick off your summer with a **family carillon picnic** at the Chicago Botanic Garden. Each Monday evening from late June to mid-August, the Butz Memorial Carillon Concert Series brings a different professional carillonneur to the carillon bell tower. From your picnic blanket on the South Lawn (the only time picnics are allowed outside the garden's official picnic area), you can survey the green acres of the garden and enjoy the gentle music of this unique instrument. Picnic concerts begin at 7:00 P.M.; tours of the carillon bell tower are available at 6:00 P.M. ([708] 835-5440)

Commemorate the 1863 abolition of slavery by celebrating **Juneteenth** at the Chicago Historical Society, where actors bring abolitionists, slaves, and owners to life on the Saturday closest to June 19. Don't miss the monologue of escaped slave Susan Boggs, who relates her experiences as a slave, tells why she decided to escape, and shares hair-raising details about what she did and

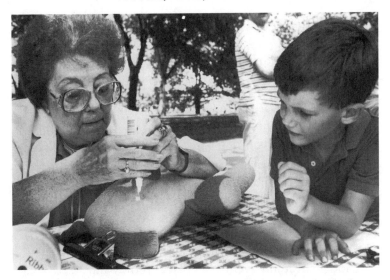

A Brookfield Zoo volunteer helps a young visitor repair his teddy bear at the Quick-Well Clinic during the Teddy Bear Picnic. *Photo by the Chicago Zoological Society.*

where she ran. Frederick Douglass, Harriet Beecher Stowe, and other historical figures also attend, and a portion of the famous Lincoln-Douglas debates on slavery are reenacted. (642-4600)

The closest thing to an old-fashioned patriotic **Fourth of July** is also held at the Chicago Historical Society. While a band plays patriotic numbers, the world's tallest Uncle Sam leads kids in a costume parade around the grounds (hint: he's on stilts). When craft activities, the music, and the parade come to an end, the Eighth Regiment Afoot brings the festivities to a close by firing authentic Brown Bess muskets from the Revolutionary War. (642-4600)

Skip the crowds at the downtown Fourth of July **fireworks** and enjoy the private display set off by the Saddle & Cycle Club (909 W. Foster Avenue, 275-6600). This tony and exclusive club won't let you in without a sponsor and a $10,000 initiation fee, but you can enjoy the show by stretching out your blankets in the park between the Sheridan Road high rises and Lake Shore Drive. (Enter the park on Berwyn Avenue, or on Foster next to

Lake Shore Drive.) You can park at Dominick's or on an adjoining residential street.

Rain or shine, the show starts at dusk. If there's a shower, watch from your car. Rain makes the fireworks explode at a slightly lower altitude and with a little less energy, but the colors and designs are still marvelous.

The Chicago Children's Museum **International Children's Fest** introduces kids to our city's great diversity. The day-long festival lets kids watch dance and hear music from a dozen cultures, and try their hands at Greek weaving, origami, sign language, mask making, and other activities. About two dozen booths offer arts and crafts from different cultures, and performances occur every twenty minutes. All of the action takes place on Navy Pier in late July. (527-1000)

Another great July event takes place on the ballfield at Wrigley Field. During the All Star break, the Cubs sponsor the **All Star Kids Clinic**, a day of sports and fun for 4- to 16-year-old kids. Older kids can attend baseball clinics with Cubs players; younger kids can play catch, run bases, or have their faces painted. Everybody takes home a goodie bag brimming with prizes, baseball hats and cards, and other souvenirs. (404-4064)

The Brookfield Zoo offers two great summer events: **Alfie the Elephant's birthday party,** held every June (watch her devour an enormous cake!), and the August **Teddy Bear Picnic,** when the favorite teddies of 25,000 Chicagoans are feted during a two-day party. Your kids can bring their teddy bears in for a checkup at the Teddy Bear Quickwell Clinic (minor repairs can be made if needed), join the teddy bear parade led by the zoo's team of Clydesdales, and enter the competition for best-dressed, most snuggled, most original, and largest stuffed bear. (There's also a category for "bear that most closely resembles its owner.") ([708] 485-0263)

Great Japanese food, fascinating martial arts displays and raucous drumming will delight your kids at the August **Ginza Festival**, sponsored by the Midwest Buddhist Temple in Old Town. After a wonderful supper of chicken teriyaki, your family can pull up a chair for an hour of noisy, exciting taiko drumming. This traditional style of drumming is guaranteed to enthrall any kid—especially when the Minneapolis and Chicago taiko groups face off against each other in a traditional "battle of the bands" that really ups the intensity. Before the drumming begins, a great judo demonstration pits tiny 4-year-olds against 250-pound black belts—with some very surprising outcomes!

The festival also showcases the old-world skills of the Waza craftsmen, who make intricate toys, brushes, dolls, and scrolls. If you buy a top, the toy maker will let your child paint it. He'll operate the lathe and help your child make incredibly delicate stripes of bright colors. (943-7801)

To immerse your family in the Renaissance, take a field trip to the August **Bristol Renaissance Faire** in Bristol, Wisconsin. The admission fee is steep, but once your family is inside, you'll be thrown into the days of knights, ladies, lords, and squires. Particularly for kids under 6, this event blurs the line between fact and fiction. They'll be amazed at the characters who pass them by: drunken, shouting knights; silent mimes and silly jesters; jolly friars and haunting, black-robed penitents. Besides the impromptu street theater, there are plenty of plays, magic shows, crafts, and games to enjoy—plus dozens of hearty meals and snacks.

When you're tired of walking, take your little kids to the cool, shaded wading pond, where they can play with simple wooden boats. Older kids can cool their heels during the exciting jousting match between the black and the red knights. And everyone can enjoy throwing wet sponges at Mom or Dad in the stocks! All in all, the Bristol Renaissance Faire makes for a fun day in the sixteenth century. ([708] 395-7773)

Medieval knights and ladies are also on hand during the August **Oz Park Festival**, which draws mimes and jugglers, stilt walkers, folk dancers, and famous folks like Garfield Goose to this two-day children's festival. Kids can enjoy the marvelous Robert Leathers playground, take in performances by local theater, dance, and music groups, or just hang out and enjoy a snow cone. (880-5200)

Fall

Get autumn off to an arty start by visiting **Around the Coyote**, Wicker Park's annual celebration of artists and their studios. Kids who love to make arts and crafts will enjoy this chance to take a privileged peek inside the studios of real artists. Have lunch at the celebrated Busy Bee Restaurant (1550 N. Damen Avenue, 772-4433) for a look at its photo gallery of famous Chicago politicians and buildings, and then pick up a map of artist's studios from the Flatiron Building at Damen and Milwaukee Avenues. Besides visiting studios, you can see a juried art show, and enjoy plenty of theater and performance art—all in one of Chicago's great neighborhoods. (342-6777)

Snakes alive! On **Herpetological Weekend**, the Chicago Herpetological Society brings its cold-blooded members to the Chicago Academy of Sciences. This is your kid's chance to meet more than a hundred live reptiles—including a 200-pound, sixteen-foot-long python—and learn more about the role these animals play in our ecosystem. Because there's always a photographer on hand, Grandma can get a picture of a python wrapped around her pride and joy. (549-0606)

Did Columbus really discover America? Among the many groups who emphatically disagree are the Swedes, who celebrate **Viking Day** instead. On the Saturday closest to Columbus Day, the Swedish American Museum invites kids to dress up as Vikings, rub runestones, make Viking jewelry (OK, it's tinfoil) and clamber over the Viking ship in the basement children's exhibit. (728-8111)

Fall is powwow time—and Chicago's biggest powwow is the November **American Indian Center of Chicago Pow Wow**. Hundreds of Native Americans from tribes all over the country participate in this event, which features Native American foods, crafts, and competitive dancing, drumming, and singing. During the dazzling Grand March that kicks off each evening's program, the participants file into the arena in their finery. It's a unique opportunity to learn about tribal costumes, purchase Native American crafts, and sample fry bread and corn soup. (275-5871)

Two other institutions that sponsor powwows are NAES College (761-5000) and the Forest Preserve District of Cook County, whose **Pow Wow** and **Primitive Skills Exhibition** is held in September in Thatcher Woods in River Forest. ([708] 771-1014)

Several institutions celebrate the fall with Harvest Festivals. At North Park Village Nature Center's two-day **Fall Harvest Festival**, your kids can decorate pumpkins, bob for apples, and roast marshmallows over a bonfire in the forest. They can also vie for prizes to create the best scarecrow! (742-5472)

The theme of the Botanic Garden's October **Harvest Festival** is apples. Kids can attend a birthday party for Johnny Appleseed, make apple butter, and learn how to save apple seeds for planting. Because the Botanic Garden's festival is scheduled to coincide with Sukkoth, the Jewish harvest holiday, the festival includes a "sukkah", a temporary shelter constructed so a family can eat at least one meal a day outdoors during the holiday. ([708] 835-5440)

Halloween

Shopping for **the perfect Halloween costume** is easy when you visit one of Chicago's costume emporia: Izzy Rizzy's House of Tricks (6034 S. Pulaski Road, 735-7370), Fantasy Headquarters (4065 N. Milwaukee Avenue, 777-0222), and A Lost Era (1511 W. Howard Street, 764-7400).

Each of these stores is bursting with costumes for rent or sale. Their A–Z list of costumes starts with "Angel," ends with "Zorro," and includes crash dummies, nuns, pirates, vampires, Bill and Hillary Rodham Clinton, and hundreds more. Don't miss the mountains of noses, beaks, mustaches, crowns, tiaras, mouse and elephant ears, antlers, and hundreds of other finishing touches. (Izzy Rizzy's also stocks tasteless kid props like pretend vomit and dog poop, Whoopee! cushions, and fake plaster casts.)

When the costume is purchased, where can kids wear it? Try **Mummies' Night** at the Oriental Institute, where kids can enjoy mummy-related craft projects, trick or treat, refreshments, and see the classic, *Abbott and Costello Meet the Mummy*. (702-9514)

The Brookfield Zoo's **Boo! at the Zoo** attracts 30,000 young visitors during its two days. There's a costume parade, a costume contest, animal games and spooky activities, and trick or treating: kids get treats if they answer an animal question correctly. ([708] 485-0263)

During the Lincoln Park Zoo's **Spooky Zoo Spectacular**, the zoo gives out more than a million pieces of candy—no questions asked! Bring your costumed kids at noon so they can join in a parade led by Bozo the Clown and Ronald McDonald. After the parade, kids can trick or treat to their hearts' content at the various animal houses. (742-7695)

When you plan your family's Halloween outing, consider your child's tolerance for fright. Beware the really scary haunted houses, where teens often consider it their duty to torment little kids to tears. (Being ushered out the fire door with a screaming child really wrecks a family outing.) With young kids, it's better to stick with events that are only mildly atmospheric, like the Forest Preserve District of Cook County's **Haunted Forest**.

During this six-night special event, nearly a mile of trails in Caldwell Woods is transformed into twenty scary scenes your child can view from a safe distance. In one scene, a witch laughs as she stirs her cauldron; at the river, you can see bloodthirsty pirates and the Grim Reaper. Other scenes star Frankenstein, gorillas, and a haunted graveyard. No one tries to chase, touch, or frighten your family. When the trail ends, kids can enjoy hot chocolate and refreshments in the witch's tent. ([708] 771-1014)

For a multicultural Halloween, make a pilgrimage to the Mexican Fine Arts Museum's annual *Dia de los Muertes* exhibit, which tells how dead relatives are enticed back to their families on All Souls Day, November 2. The exhibit features altars built to tempt the deceased with their favorite food and drink, items of clothing, family pictures, tools and objects.

A macabre touch is added by the hundreds of skeletons in the exhibit. Made from clay, metal, and paper, they are dressed as organ grinders, knife sharpeners, bakers, doctors, bicycle delivery men, and other just plain folks. Be sure to watch the video explaining the significance of the holiday and the rituals that celebrate it, and treat your kids to an inexpensive sugar skeleton from the gift shop. (738-1503)

Hanukkah, Christmas, and Kwanzaa

Don't want to start your Christmas shopping the day after Thanksgiving? Then head to the Art Institute instead. The holiday season kicks off at 10:00 A.M., when the Institute's lions don wreaths, and three days of continuous family art activities begin. Stop by to see artists demonstrating their skills, listen to enthralling stories, and make and take inspired art projects. (443-3680)

While you're in the Loop, don't forget to stroll down State Street to see Field's and Carson's animated Christmas window displays. Whether you shop or not, it's a fun day to be downtown.

Animated Christmas windows are a dime a dozen, but to see an animated Hanukkah display, drop by Fluky's Hot Dogs (6821 N. Western Avenue, 274-3652). Your kids can also make a family menorah at one of the Spertus Museum's Menorah workshops. (922-9012)

Christmas in Sweden starts on December 13, the feast of Santa Lucia, when children, led by the oldest daughter, serve their parents rolls and coffee in bed. The children dress in white robes and the oldest daughter dons a wreath of candles, bringing welcome light to a murky Swedish morning.

At the Swedish American Museum, **Santa Lucia Day** is a big deal. Starting at 5:00 P.M., a bevy of carolers sings its way up and down Clark Street, returning to the museum for juice, coffee, and Swedish gingersnaps and songs. After refreshments, the gaily decorated museum dims the lights and more than a dozen young Lucias parade through, candles blazing on their heads.

After more refreshments and a visit from Santa, families can walk over to Ebenezer Lutheran Church, where the bilingual Santa Lucia service packs this lovely Swedish American church to the rafters. If your kids can sit still for the service, they'll be rewarded by beautiful Swedish hymns, an address by the Swedish

Cast and puppets lead a rousing reveille during the Redmoon Theater's annual Winter Pageant. *Courtesy Redmoon Theater.*

consulate, another candlelight procession, and more gingersnaps and coffee afterward! (728-8111)

Kids can get a taste of yesterday's Christmas at three local historical houses. On the first three Saturdays of December, the Frank Lloyd Wright Home and Studio offers free Victorian tours (led by the Studio's middle-school-age Junior Interpreters) from 9:00 to 11:00 A.M. The Home and Studio also offers kids-only **Victorian Christmas parties** selected evenings in December. During the party, kids make crafts typical of the turn of the century, sing carols, enjoy refreshments, and put on a play in the playroom. Parties are available for children in kindergarten through sixth grade. ([708] 848-1978)

On Chicago's South Prairie Avenue, kids can learn how Christmas was celebrated in the nineteenth century. In the Glessner House, decorated for the 1890s, the walls and doors are festooned with Victorian swags and decorations and the two Christmas trees are lavishly adorned with nineteenth-century ornaments. The trees feature lights instead of candles because the Glessners were among the first to use electric tree lights, as the family's journals and letters attest.

Because the 1836 Clarke House was built before the Christmas tree became an American institution, it is more simply dressed up for a New Year's Day reception. Both houses can be visited during the first two weekends in December, when they are illuminated with candles and docents explain how their former occupants celebrated the holidays. Many of the details concern the rituals of the Glessner children, like the "Christmas pie" of toys buried in rice or sand. The two-hour evening tours spend an hour in each house, so if your child gets impatient, you can leave the tour after visiting just one. (326-1949)

During **Holiday Magic**, the Brookfield Zoo's holiday celebration, half a million white lights turn the zoo's park into a winter wonderland. These evening celebrations, which take place December weekends from 4:00 to 9:00 P.M., include singing to the animals, strolling carolers, ice carving, storytelling, crafts, and a tree-decorating party. Of course, Santa is on hand every night to hear holiday wishes. ([708] 485-0263)

On the first weekend in December, the Lincoln **Park Free-for-All Holiday Party in the Park** kicks off with Caroling to the Animals at the Lincoln Park Zoo. The songfest begins around the Sea Lion pool as Santa Claus feeds his flippered friends and carolers join a rousing chorus of "Jingle Bells." Kids can follow Santa on his rounds to the animal houses, or stroll at their own pace with their families. At every animal house, complimentary cider and cookies are served.

After the caroling, families can walk over to the Chicago Academy of Sciences to enjoy the music of a local children's choir and make an environmentally friendly ornament. The Party in the Park ends with a special tree-lighting ceremony in front of the museum. (549-0606)

Another kind of light shines at the Adler Planetarium, whose **Star of Wonder** sky show lets your family see what the wisemen saw over Bethlehem. Was it an exploding star, a comet, or an unusual meeting of the planets? To answer the question, Star of Wonder examines the night skies of Bethlehem in 2 and 3 B.C.

Two institutions let your family learn about holiday traditions around the world. The Museum of Science and Industry's *Christmas Around the World* exhibit displays dozens of Christmas trees, each decorated by a different community group to reflect its ethnic traditions. Ornament-making workshops and music and dance performances near the trees bring each culture's Christmas rituals to life.

The museum's *Holidays of Light* exhibit expands the holiday spirit to encompass other traditions of the season, including Kwanzaa, Hanukkah, Diwali, Ramadan, Chinese New Year, and Santa Lucia Day. (684-1414)

The Kohl Children's Museum also uses performances and craft activities to celebrate December holidays from around the globe. Kids can make a good luck design to celebrate the Hindu holiday Diwali; build a lotus boat like the ones floated along waterways during the Thai holiday Loy Krathong; participate in a Santa Lucia procession or play an animal in a Mexican posada play; build a star lantern to celebrate the Filipino Cock Crow Mass; or make candles for menorahs and ornaments for Christmas. The Kohl even celebrates the British holiday Boxing Day on the day after Christmas!

During the last week of December, the Kohl Children's Museum celebrates the African American holiday Kwanzaa by letting children design a mkeka (place mat) and make a kinara (candle holder). Storytellers also visit the museum to regale kids with wonderful African folktales and inspiring African American stories. ([708] 256-3000)

Druids can celebrate the solstice at North Park Village's Winter Solstice Party, where marshmallows and chestnuts are roasted over an open campfire and kids can make solstice cards and edible ornaments: one to take home, and one to leave behind for nature center residents. Naturalists talk about the solstice's meteorological and cultural significance, and give tours through the nature center's acreage. (742-5472)

Many families make a ritual of two seasonal cultural events: the Nutcracker ballet at the Arie Crown Theater, and the Goodman Theater's Christmas Carol. (For tickets, call Ticketmaster, 902-1500.)

When Christmas and Hanukkah are over, the Art Institute of Chicago throws open its doors for **Holly Days**. On the four days between Christmas and New Year, the Institute offers a busy schedule of art activities, games, and story hours for families with the we're-tired-of-the-holidays blues. (443-3600)

End the year or start the new one at Redmoon Theater's **Winter Pageant** in Logan Square. Using only snippets of dialogue—signs pinned to clotheslines or chants taken from singles ads—this dreamlike meditation on life tells its tale with larger-than-life papier-mâché puppets, people on stilts, buskers playing all manner of instruments and noisemakers, and fast-changing sets and costumes.

While the under-6 set may be intimidated by the oversize characters and their surreal actions, older kids and teens will marvel at the pageant, envy the children in its cast. (They'll probably want to stage a show just like it in your very own living room.) And like all great literature and theater, the pageant's theme of rebirth and renewal ends on a hopeful note, confirming the essential meaning of our lives. (772-9069)

Index

Other Chicago-Area Guidebooks from Chicago Review Press

The Chicago Arts Guide
June Skinner Sawyers and Sue Telingator
"As thorough as one could want . . . a load of information, thoughtfully gathered and organized." —Dick Kogan
Chicago Tribune

456 pages, 6 x 9
paper, $12.95
ISBN 1-55652-162-6

Chicago on Foot
Walking Tours of Chicago's Architecture
Fifth Edition
Ira J. Bach and Susan Wolfson
Revised and updated by James Cornelius
This classic guide includes 31 tours with maps and directions designed for walkers.
360 pages, 8 x 10
paper, $14.95
ISBN 1-55652-209-6

Chicago's Museums
A Complete Guide to the City's Cultural Attractions
Revised Edition
Victor Danilov
A comprehensive guide to Chicago's museums, zoos, botanical gardens, and other cultural attractions.
304 pages, 5½ x 8½
paper, $11.95
ISBN 1-55652-135-9

Norman Mark's Chicago
Walking Bicycling & Driving Tours of the City
Fourth Edition
Norman Mark
An entertaining way to explore the architectural, cultural, and historical highlights of Chicago.
392 pages, 6 x 9
paper, $12.95
ISBN 1-55652-197-9

Somewhere Over the Dan Ryan
Day and Weekend Outings for Chicago-Area Families
Revised & Expanded
Joanne Y. Cleaver
Offers short-term family outings in Illinois, Wisconsin, Michigan, Indiana, and Missouri. Includes an index of sights and activities, indicating free attractions.
232 pages, 5½ x 8½
paper, $11.95
ISBN 1-55652-180-4

Sweet Home Chicago
The Real City Guide
Fourth Edition
Revised & Expanded
Edited by Amy Teschner
An unpretentious, streetwise, easy-going guide to Chicago.
486 pages, 6 x 9
paper, $11.95
ISBN 1-55652-161-8

Twain, Plains & Automobile
Driving Tours Through the Historical Midwest
Joanne Y. Cleaver
Unique theme tours through Wisconsin, Illinois, Michigan, Ohio, Kentucky, Missouri, and Indiana.
288 pages, 5½ x 8½
paper, $11.95
ISBN 1-55652-210-X